Gail Worstman's Goodtime
HARDTIMES COOKBOOK

By Gail L. Worstman

Gray Beard Publishing

Seattle, Washington

©1982 Gail L. Worstman

Illustrations ©1982 Gregg Scott

All rights reserved. No part of this book may be reproduced or transmitted in any form or by any means, electronic or mechanical, including photocopying, recording or information storage and retrieval systems now known or to be invented, without permission in writing from the publisher, except that brief passages may be quoted for reviews.

Printed in the United States of America.

Library of Congress Catalog Card Number: 82-81587

ISBN-0-933686-01-3

Gray Beard Publishing
107 West John St.
Seattle, Washington 98119
(206) 285-3171

Cover design: Ben Dennis
Cover photo: Ben Dennis
Book design: Ben Dennis, Gregg Scott
Typestyles: Clearface and Century Old Style,
　　set by Janis Kaleem and Kim Field

Special thanks for the front cover to Meg Russell, Hasson Brothers Produce of Pike Place Market, Magnolia Kitchen Shoppe of Seattle and Keith Worstman.

*To Sunrise And
The Land Where The
Rainbow Begins*

Contents

Introduction	7
Do It Yourself (Sprouting, Drying)	9
Appetizers, Beverages, Condiments	37
Soup, Sauces	51
Salads, Dressing	65
Main Dishes (Fish, Meat, Vegetable)	77
Side Dishes	91
Cookies, Cakes, Pies, Frostings	103
Breads (Yeast, Quick, Cereals)	117
Desserts (Treats, Puddings, Ice Cream)	131
Herbs (Terminology, Herbs, Recipes)	139
U.S./Metric Conversion Chart	152
Index	154
Notes	158

Introduction

To eat well during a difficult economy takes a little thought, a few tricks and a bit of work.

Some advance plannning, seasonal shopping and a willingness to wait an extra half hour before eating will open a new horizon in dining for you and your family.

Along with tasty cuisine, this book will also show you how to make simple foods you are paying high prices for at the store. Foods like yogurt, sour cream, cream cheese, pasta, pastries, creme fraiche and sprouts will save you at least half if not up to 5 times the cost when made from scratch. Simple foods, without the usual mess and fuss.

Learn also how to dehydrate fruits and vegetables. Canning and freezing of foods is simple too, given a few shortcuts. Make jerky, mayonnaise, relish, salsa and more. Cut corners, calories and cost by making soups and casseroles in a thermos bottle. Yes, even cut energy consumption while saving elsewhere in the kitchen as well.

The result: fresh foods prepared well, with an eye toward monthly bargains and a sense of economy and nutrition combined for premium taste.

Invite your family...invite yourself to feast and celebrate. A toast to Goodtimes!

DO IT YOURSELF

Make Bread

Expression of love for those you care for.

The aroma of freshly baked bread sends a message of love to those you care for. It may be an easy expression of love for you, or it can be a long journey through hockey-puck heaven without a few hot tips to help you.

Properly milled, high protein flour is necessary for perfect rising and texture. A low protein, coarse flour will fail you as many of my friends have discovered by purchasing "whole wheat flour" in the grocery store. Much of it is degermed, not stone-ground and made of low quality wheat. Shop around for freshly milled, high protein flour.

When dissolving yeast, use warm water which you would wash your face (but not your hands) in. Include a teaspoon of honey or other sweetener called for and let it stand 10 minutes before proceeding. If you do not wish to sweeten your bread, add ¼ teaspoon ground ginger to the yeast. It will work perfectly and will not flavor your baked product.

Kneading is generally the procedure which scares most would-be breadmakers. Kneading is a working of the dough with the hands to exercise and develop the gluten for proper rising. When kneading, keep your hands flattened. Do not squish the dough. Have flour on the table and flour on your hands to prevent sticking. Always work toward making the dough into a smooth ball. Most kneading for a 1-2 loaf recipe will be complete in 7-10 minutes. The dough will decline in its rate of flour absorption and will eventually stop taking flour. That is generally the time to stop. If you must continue to knead, oil your hands and the board and continue in that manner.

Keep hands flat.
Do not squish dough.

Let your dough rise in an oiled, covered bowl until double in bulk. Punch it down with your fist, turn it in the bowl, then shape loaves with the dough. Place dough in oiled pans and cover to let rise again. Only rise until double in bulk. Temptation to have your loaf on the cover of a magazine may cause you to let it rise above its level of competence. In the oven an over-risen loaf falls flat. Only rise to double in bulk and it will rise a bit more in the oven. (Note: for fast bread shape dough directly into baking pans and rise until double only once. Pop into oven and bake as directed. The texture will be more open, but in the interests of saving time, and the phenomenal trick of serving fresh bread for dinner, this can be tried.) Rising time is generally 45 minutes, depending upon the warmth of the place chosen. Avoid rising in chilly or drafty areas. A water heater, oven with a pilot light or by a radiating heater are all great places for rising. Always cover rising dough with a towel.

Bake in oiled pans in the center of a moderately hot oven. Bread is done when a hollow sound is detected by thumping the top of a loaf. If your loaf is done on the outside, yet dough on the inside then your oven is too hot. If you want a shiny or glazed loaf, always brush on a glaze before the final rising. For a soft crust, brush the finished loaf with butter or oil as it comes out of the oven.

Cool bread in the pan for 3-5 minutes, on its side on a wire rack. Then remove the loaf and continue cooling on its side on the wire rack. When fully cooled, wrap and store. If you can wait to slice until the next day it will be easier. Of course, at my house I am lucky to get a loaf into the freezer! Double-wrapped, that is.

Pantry Bread

Just as there is refrigerator soup, so too there is pantry bread. With the popular formula for a loaf of bread you can invent your own recipe for a wonderful loaf of custom crunch. Here is the basic ratio of ingredients:

1½ to 2 cups liquid ingredients
  includes: oil, eggs, honey, molasses, milk, yogurt, juice or water
2 teaspoons yeast
  dissolve this in ¼ cup of warm liquid, plus 1 teaspoon sweetener.
4½ to 6 cups flour
  includes basic flour, plus milk powder, brewers yeast, soy flour, buckwheat flour, sprouts, grain meal and dry herbs
1 teaspoon sea salt, added with first flour

Combine the yeast mixture with the remaining wet ingredients and stir well. Add in about ⅔ of the dry ingredients and stir well. (At this time, all but the basic flour in the recipe must be incorporated.) Add the remaining flour in gradually, then pour onto a floured board and knead until the dough is smooth and elastic and not sticky. Let rise in an oiled, covered bowl until double in bulk. Punch down, shape and place in oiled pan for rising to double again. Bake at 350-375 for 35-55 minutes, depending upon heaviness of dough and thickness of loaf. Remove and cool on wire rack, on its side.

Makes 1 unique loaf.

Make Pasta

Since Marco Polo brought noodles back to Italy from China the Western world has had a love affair with noodles. Now found in the diets of most cultures of the temperate and tropical zones, pasta in one form or another has found its way into the hearts and onto the thighs of the world.

Noodles can be found in soup, under clams, around meatballs, fried crunchy and savored cold for breakfast. And recently pasta has enjoyed a return to the kitchens of gourmets and gourmands. The difference this time is the cooks are making it themselves. A great proliferation of pasta machines, gadgets and very expensive equipment is available for this humble noodle-making. Fortunately there are a few affordable, hand-crank types which will do the job adequately (unless you want to rough it and roll the dough yourself). Before you buy a pasta machine, however, try rolling out a batch by hand, cooking and eating it first to decide if you enjoy the homemade touch. If you do then shop around and compare the different machines and their available attachments. Then select the machine that will serve your needs. If you eat a lot of pasta then having a machine will certainly make life a little easier.

Be aware that the pasta people will not be encouraging you to use whole grain flours. They will generally recommend semolina flour, a refined soft wheat flour. And for white pasta I suggest you use it. You can insure whole grain goodness, however, by using whole wheat pastry flour. Simply adapt your recipe by removing 1 tablespoon whole wheat pastry flour from every cup called for in the pasta recipe.

Vegetable pasta, such as spinach, carrot, artichoke and tomato are accomplished with 10-15% vegetable powder or flour. If you cannot buy these then use thick puree and adjust for the added moisture. Most vegetable pasta is enhanced with a pinch of parsley and chive, pulverized.

To make a perfect batch of pasta:

4 cups whole wheat pastry flour
2 teaspoons sea salt
4 eggs, beaten
¼ cup olive oil
⅓ cup water

Make a mound of the flour and salt and make a well in the middle. In a small bowl combine the eggs, oil and water. Pour the wet mixture into the flour well. With your hands gently mix together until a ball of dough is formed. Keep kneading until the ball is smooth and not sticky. Cover the dough with a towel and let stand for 30 minutes. Divide the dough into 8 pieces and roll to ⅛" thick. (At this point follow manufacturer's directions for a pasta rolling machine.) Let dough rest 3 minutes and continue rolling until dough is 1/16" thick. Roll each dough piece up like a jelly roll and slice the roll every ¼" (or wider if you want wider noodles). Spread the noodles out to dry on a lightly floured surface and let stand uncovered for at least 1 hour. The noodles are now ready to be cooked for a meal. Boil in water until al dente ('to the teeth', meaning noodles which have body when chewed). Drain and dress.

Serves 6.

To prepare for future use, continue drying noodles several more hours, then wrap and freeze for later use.

Pasta recipes have endless options for flavor and accent. Use vegetable juice, powdered herbs and vegetables and various oils to vary this basic recipe. Ground sesame seeds, small amounts of rice flour, corn flour, rye or buckwheat flour will add variety as well. For a more primitive effect use whole wheat flour. For added nutrition, include a bit of protein powder or brewer's yeast. In any case, enjoy!

Can Your Own Fruit

The benefits of putting up your own fruit start with solid nutritional value, include no sugar and definitely have fewer calories. The fresher taste and personal satisfaction complete my reasons for going to "all the trouble." Actually I have discovered that doing one batch an evening while making dinner adds up to a full pantry very quickly, and allows for canning only the ripest fruits on a working person's schedule. So we get lots of wonderful food without the back-breaking marathon canning weekends I remember from my childhood.

Three basic solutions can be used with fruits: canning with honey, apple juice or straight water. Using water has only one trick to it. Measure out the approximate amount of water you will use and let it stand overnight open to the air, but protected from debris. This will allow any chlorine or fluorine to evaporate rather than end up in your peaches.

When canning with honey, make a solution depending upon the amount of sweetness you normally enjoy:

light syrup: 1 cup honey to 4 cups boiling water

medium syrup: 2 cups honey to 4 cups boiling water

heavy syrup: 3 cups honey to 4 cups boiling water

Fill scalded jars with raw fruits, then fill with liquid to 1½" of the top of the jar. Seal and process in a hot water bath according to the fruit used.

Canning with apple juice is less expensive and not as 'sweet' tasting as honey. It offers a non-specific sweetness, while some stronger honeys may offer additional flavoring you are not interested in. For canning with an apple juice solution, use apple juice concentrate (frozen apple juice concentrate is the easiest form) and follow this chart for desired sweetness:

thin syrup: 1 cup apple juice concentrate to 8 cups water

medium syrup: 1 cup apple juice concentrate to 6 cups water

heavy syrup: 1 part apple juice concentrate to 4 cups water

Always select unsweetened juice for this, and remember that an 'unstrained or old fashioned' variety may be cloudy.

When processing in a hot water bath in quart jars, follow these times for the fruits indicated:

apples	20 minutes
applesauce	10
apricots	20
berries	15
cherries	25
peaches	25
pears	25
plums	25
rhubarb	10
fruit juices	5
fruit purees or spreads	10

Freezing Your Own Fruit

To freeze fruits with syrup choose a medium or heavy syrup. Chill your mixed syrup before combining with prepared fruit, then fill your freezer containers to ½" of the top. Seal, label and freeze, unstacked, in a 0 degree Fahrenheit freezer. Your frozen foods will retain maximum freshness for 9-12 months at this temperature.

Making Your Own Jam

When making fast cooking jam with a favorite recipe, an easy substitution of honey or apple juice concentrate will get you out of the sugar rut. Roughly 1 cup honey or apple juice concentrate may be used for every 4 cups of mashed fruit. Adjust for your personal taste or thickness desired.

Making Your Own Juice

Juice can be extracted from fruits with a juicing machine, by pressing and with a juicer-steamer. All work with excellent results when the proper fruits for which they were designed are used. Consult the directions for the juices that do well before starting. Being creative with juice combinations is also fun. Apple juice mixes well with most berries. Experiment with your own tastebuds and decide on the combinations before canning. Sweeten with apple juice, pear juice or honey before sealing.

A Word About Canning

Make sure your jars, lids and rings are in perfect condition. Examine each jar lip and discard any jar with a chip or other imperfection. Make sure each lid has a perfect seal. Examine the rings for dents and rust, keeping only the perfect ones. Make sure each lid seals properly by tapping with a spoon no earlier than 4 hours after processing. Reprocess any unsealed fruits, or if there are only a few store in the refrigerator and consume within a few days. If you have a big sealing problem, document it and the cost of your loss due to poor rings, jars or whatever and discuss it with the store owner who sold you the defective items. A canning disaster is very expensive and time is your most critical ingredient. With the return of canning as a domestic activity the quality of some canning implements can be affected in a peak season.

Can Your Own Vegetables

The rewards of a successful garden are shown in the vegetables which are preserved for the winter to come. Vegetable canning is a bit more time-consuming and costly, since a pressure cooker is necessary. My technique of doing one batch of canning per evening is especially suited to vegetables since pressure cooking is so much more tedious. Cold packing of the 'easier' vegetables takes a load off the process, though. (Cold packing is recommended only for asparagus, Lima beans, snap beans, corn, carrots, peas and zucchini.)

All other vegetables must be hot packed (cooked in advance of filling the jars) because of their alkalinity. And they all need a pressure-cooker processing. Please avoid canning the following vegetables: cabbage (except sauerkraut), cauliflower, celery, cucumbers (except pickles), baked beans, eggplant, lettuce, onions, parsnips, turnips and vegetable mixes (except pickled).

The following chart reflects cooking time for vegetables packed in 1 quart jars at 10 pounds pressure:

asparagus	30 minutes
beans (green or wax)	25
beans, lima	50
beets	35
carrots	30
corn, whole kernel	85
corn, cream-style	95
greens (spinach, beet, collard)	90
mushrooms	35
peas	40
potatoes, white	40
pumpkin and winter squash	80
summer squash	40

Make Candied Fruit and Garnishes

Finding healthful alternatives for festive holiday baking is not all that easy. I have even been known from time to time to break a rule or two and go for the chemically colored and heavily sugared fruits. Now the choice is clear, and quick. Make your own baking fruits! Not only whole fruits for baking, either, but crunchy garnishes for desserts and toppings. The following recipe will work for any fruit or fruit peel you wish to glaze. Try cherries, pineapple, orange peel slices and slivers, lemon or lime and even kumquat. For citrus peel, slice to 1/8" thick. For citrus garnish, sliver slice at 1/2" long by paper-thin.

1 cup honey
1/2 cup water
1 cup prepared fruit or peel

Combine the honey and water in a shallow saucepan and bring to the boil for 2 minutes. Lower the temperature to simmer and add in the fruit. Stir gently and simmer about 10 minutes. Remove the fruit to cool on cooking parchment or wire racks. (Do not use waxed paper or aluminum foil. If you have a marble slab, that is perfect.)

Makes 1 cup candied fruit.

Note: Candied slivers are ideal garnishes for ice cream or pudding desserts as well as frosted cakes, pies and pastries.

Make Sprouts

Sprouts are loaded with nutritional value. High in vitamins, minerals and chlorophyll, sprouts are the most exciting of the "fresh, whole foods." Make sure the seeds you sprout are not sprayed or treated in any way. Alfalfa seeds are a dry mustard yellow-green, mung beans are deep green, azuki beans are deep red with an aristocratic black stripe, lentils are green-brown, wheat is medium brown (no white spots or soft grain) and sunflower seeds are uniform in shape and not salted or toasted. (Remember, in the shell or unhulled sunflower seeds are sprouted in soil while out of the shell or hulled sunflower seeds are sprouted in a sprouting jar.) Other commonly sprouted seeds include radish, cabbage, peas, garbanzo beans and soybeans.

To Sprout:

Consult the chart for the amount of sprouting seeds needed for your choice. Wash seeds well in cool water, then place them in a clean quart jar with 1 cup warm water. Let stand overnight, then rinse twice and drain well. Cover the jar opening with a sprouting lid or cheesecloth secured with a rubberband. Drain again. Store in a dark place for 1-2 days, or until sprouts begin to appear. During that time rinse with warm water twice daily. When sprouts appear bring them into the daylight and continue to sprout, rinsing 3 times daily with warm water until desired length is achieved. Consult the chart for the desired length for best flavor. The best judge is your tastebuds. Remember, as the sprouts get too long they will have a stronger flavor. The smaller sprouts will be more tender.

The following sprout chart will clearly show many different seed choices, special instructions for each and characteristics of desired results. It also shares tips, nutritional information and serving suggestions.

Some seed combinations are also very tasty and offer a special touch to sprouting. When combining these seeds, achieve a visual mix the first time. Adjust for personal preference after the initial experience. For instance, combine alfalfa, wheat, lentil and hulled sunflower seeds for an excellent salad mixture. Alfalfa, radish and lentil make a great sandwich or salad combination. Garbanzo, lentil, pea, mung and wheat mix well as the base of a pocketbread filling. Wheat, alfalfa and sunflower are excellent in baked goods. (You may want to sprout, dehydrate, pulverize and add this mixture as a powder or flour. Use no more than ¼ of this when substituting for other flour in a recipe.) A hearty salad combination which will be enjoyed for years to come includes alfalfa, cabbage, lentil, mung and radish.

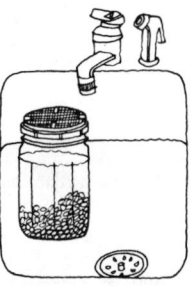 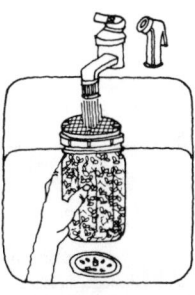 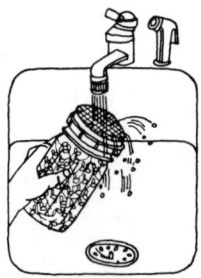

Soak your sprouting seeds or mixes overnight in jar using a screen top. Drain the following morning.

Rinse and drain your sprouts thoroughly morning and evening. Prop jar at an angle with screen top facing down, to insure proper ventilation during sprouting.

Continue rinse cycle, rinsing hulls away, until harvest time, 3 to 5 days!

Seed Sprouting Chart

SPROUTING SEED VARIETY	ALFALFA	BLACK—EYED PEAS	CABBAGE	GARBANZOS GREEN PEA
DRY SEED MEASURE	1½-2 T.	1 cup	¼ cup	¾ cup
SPROUT YIELD	1 quart	1 quart	1 quart	1 quart
SOAK TIME	4-6 hours	8-12 hours	8-12 hours	12-16 hours
SCREEN TOPS	Begin fine, change to medium	Coarse screen	Begin fine, change to medium	Coarse screen
RINSE HULLS AWAY	3rd or 4th day	No hulls	3rd or 4th day	No hulls
GROWING TIME*	4-6 days	3-4 days	4-6 days	3-5 days
HARVEST LENGTH	1-2 inches	¼-¾ inch	¾-1½ inch	½-1 inch
SPROUTING TIPS	Place in indirect sunlight 1-2 days before harvest, to develop chlorophyll	Allow ample room for expansion during soak time	Allow time to develop chlorophyll, but sharp flavor if too old	Combine with wheat for nutritious mixture
NUTRITIONAL HIGHLIGHTS	Tops list in content of minerals, protein, Vitamins A, B-complex, C, D, E, K	Protein, minerals, Vitamins A and C	Rich in minerals, Vitamins A and C	Complete protein, numerous minerals
SERVING IDEAS	Enjoy raw in salads, sandwiches	Tastes like fresh peas in a pod; delicious raw in salads	Use alone, or combine with alfalfa	Nutty flavor, good in salads, marinate them for delicious finger food

*Growing time may vary due to temperature and water conditions.

LENTILS AZUKI	JUMBO MUNG BEANS (Bean Sprouts)	RADISH	SOYBEANS	SUNFLOWER (Hulled)	WHEAT BERRIES
¾ cup	¾ cup	¼ cup	1 cup	2 cups	¾-1⅓ cups
1 quart	1 quart	1 quart	1 quart	1 quart	1 quart
8-12 hours	8-12 hours	8-12 hours	12-16 hours	8-12 hours	8-12 hours
Begin medium, change to coarse	Begin medium, change to coarse	Begin fine, change to coarse	Coarse screen	Begin medium, change to coarse	Medium screen
3rd or 4th day for seed skins	3rd or 4th day	3rd or 4th day	No hulls	3rd or 4th day for seed skins	No hulls
3-4 days	3-5 days	3-5 days	3-5 days	2-4 days	2-3 days or 4-7 days
¼-½ inch	½-2 inches	½-1½ inches	½-1 inch	Not more than ½ inch	¼-1 inch
Tasty and crispy if grown longer, but less nutritious	Grow in dark, at warmer temperature; when rinsing soak one minute before draining	Develop chlorophyll, snappy flavor, a touch of colorful red	Best sprouted alone, do not use soak water, extra rinsing desirable	Sprout will get bitter if allowed to develop green leaves	Length grown depends upon intended use
Complete protein, B vitamins	Protein, Vitamins A, C, calcium phosphorous, iron	Potassium, other minerals	Complete protein, Vitamins A, B-complex, C, E	Minerals, proteins, unsaturated fatty acids, Vitamins D and E	Good protein Vitamins B-complex C, E, complete nutrition
Delicious in soups, salads, dressings, or spreads	Omelettes, Oriental dishes, salads, soups	Salads, meat loaf, sandwiches, blend in dips	Base for cheese or yogurt, in casseroles, salads, or steam them	Delicious as is, in salads or spreads, with fruit or desserts	Short: salads, soups, casseroles Long: dessert, breads, or juice

Sprouting information and chart courtesy Sprout Ease® Bima Industries

Some sprouting is done in shallow soil. The most popular of these sprouts are sunflower, wheat grass and buckwheat. All are grown in about 2" of soil in shallow bedding boxes. Sow them under 1/8" soil, press lightly and keep wet. The sunflower sprout is ready when about 4" high and beginning to put out a second set of leaves. Snip at the base, wash and include in salads. The buckwheat is similar, snipping at 4" and rinsing off the unique hulls before serving. Wheat grass is grown for its high chlorophyll content. It is harvested at 4-5", ground in a food grinder and the juice used for cleansing diets and high energy beverages. (Do not try to juice wheat grass in a commercial juicer. It is too fibrous. A wheat grass juicer is best.)

Try sprouting as often as possible. It is by far the most economical food value. Turning a tablespoon of seeds into a quart of nutritious, fresh food is a worthwhile activity.

Sprouting increases the nutritional value of the seed involved sometimes as much as 600%, offering living, fresh food at your fingertips. Even if you lack a green thumb, sprouting is easy. You will certainly notice the extra green in your wallet!

Make Mayonnaise

That fluffy mystery in a jar that makes a turkey sandwich the heavenly delight it is contains 5 ingredients and takes a few minutes to make at home. Read your next mayo jar list of ingredients and see if you can beat that. Then check the price. Now scan below. I know we can beat the price. And for the quarts of the stuff I go through in August I want the best and the most economical I can get.

1 large egg
2 tablespoons lemon juice
¼ teaspoon sea salt
½ teaspoon dry mustard
1½ cups safflower oil

Place the first four ingredients in a blender or food processor and whip for 1 minute. Slowly drip in the oil with the blender still running until all the oil is used. Scrape the blender down twice during this process. Chill 4 hours before using. Mayonnaise will firm up during chilling.

Makes 2 cups mayo.

Variations: Every brand of mayo or 'salad dressing' on the market has its own brand of tang. That is achieved with lemon juice, vinegar and dry mustard in varying degrees. Attain your favorite flavor by combining these different ingredients in ½ teaspoonful variations until you get what you're looking for.

Rescuing the Avocado

Ever wanted just half an avocado? Or only a few slices for garnish or a moisturizing face masque? But you resisted, knowing that the rest of the avocado would go to waste if you cut into it. Well despair no longer. The magical cure for this unnecessary problem is at hand. Simply leave the pit in the portion of the avocado you are returning to the refrigerator. The avocado will not deteriorate, but will remain fresh and ripe until used later.

Fortunately this principle is also applicable to the peach, nectarine and mango. Any large-pitted fruit will behave this way, since the seed continues to communicate with the remaining fruit flesh and keep it fresh.

Make Your Own Baby Foods

The best food for babies up to a year of age is mother's milk, so the first most important baby food is the food the mother eats herself to stay healthy. Under ideal conditions a baby need not eat solid foods until its enzymes are developed to handle whole foods, usually at 12 months of age. Many parents begin to feed their babies solid foods earlier, and if this is necessary or desired then the first appropriate foods are grains such as rice and barley and fruits such as bananas or unsweetened applesauce.

When preparing grains for a baby, cook the grains in triple the ordinary water and cook until smooth. If possible, soak grains overnight before cooking since this will increase the nutritional value as well. Never season baby food with salt or spices, and never sweeten baby food.

Raw banana or raw or cooked apple are easy fruits and fast favorites for babies. Mash and feed fresh and unsweetened. Also, when exploring the new world of foods with your baby, introduce no more than one new food every week or two. This will help you identify any allergies.

Vegetables may be introduced as purees. Steam, bake or boil and then mash or puree unseasoned vegetables.

More complicated proteins should be held back until the first molars appear. This is normally a good sign that the stomach enzymes are ready to handle animal protein.

To make baby feeding times easier, making up larger batches and freezing them in ice cube trays may help. Preserving in smaller jars may also work. Remember, however, that variety is not really a vital concern for the baby. Oatmeal, bananas and peas, together with milk will keep a baby perfectly happy for a week or two. The parents may find this boring, but no sense working extra hard just for an inconsequential change of scenery!

I highly recommend the baby food grinder, available from a number of companies. It is light, versatile and easy to handle. Use it at your table and feed the baby what you are having by grinding it up for her/him fresh on the spot. Especially handy when traveling, this little gadget offers baby fresh whole foods without special preparation.

Some baby food companies are beginning to respond to the need for more natural baby foods, but they have not reached any pinnacles of perfection in my opinion. With salt, sugar, modified food starch and other indigestible or non-nutritive additions to baby's food still evident, they have a long way to go to equal the food value found in home cooking with whole foods.

Make Yogurt

Saving three-fourths of the cost of a staple food item has always been enough reason for me to make something at home, and with plain yogurt you can save a bundle. It's so easy, you'll wonder why you haven't been doing it all along. This recipe is universal and will make a thick, creamy yogurt. It will work whether you have yogurt-making equipment or an earthen bowl and a large wool blanket. For yogurt starter select a natural commercial brand without additives. This may be a packet of dry culture or it may be a container of plain yogurt. Make sure the bacteria *L. acidophilus, L. bulgaricus* and *Streptococcus thermophilus* are present. A raw milk yogurt will generally have a good selection of these bacteria, as will a raw milk goat yogurt.

4 cups milk
  (skim, 2% or whole milk will all work)
¼ cup powdered milk
¼ cup plain yogurt for starter
  (or per dry packet directions)

Combine milk and milk powder in a blender and whip until smooth. Pour into a saucepan and heat to the boiling point, but DO NOT BOIL. Remove from the heat and cool partially. Test the milk for proper warmth by sprinkling a bit on your wrist. When it feels warm but not hot to the wrist then add in the plain yogurt and stir until it is completely included. Pour into an earthen bowl (warmed) and wrap with a woolen blanket. Place in a box and stuff newspaper around it. Place the box in a warm area (by the waterheater or near a stove, or in an oven with a pilot light) for about 3-6 hours or overnight. Unwrap and refrigerate. Before consuming, reserve ¼ cup of this yogurt for your next batch.

Makes about 4½ cups yogurt.

Hints for Making Yogurt:

For a lower calorie yogurt, use skim milk and non-fat powdered milk. The yogurt will be creamier as the fat content increases. Consider, however, the vitamin A in the milk fat before going completely fat-free.

For fruited yogurt, only add fruits, jams, jellies or other goodies to yogurt as it is being served. Never make yogurt with juice or fruit in it. The fruits interfere with the liveliness of the culture. Consider this also when buying commercial yogurt. The most advantageous commercial yogurt is plain yogurt with fruits on the bottom. There is even one variety with fruit separate. They get the gold star for effort in offering a first-rate product.

Be most careful when heating the milk. If the milk boils, the yogurt will have a very strong taste. Also, when the yogurt is incubating, maintain a temperature between 105-112 Fahrenheit (40-44 Celsius). This will insure fast culturing and will be the best of conditions. Using a yogurt machine is the surest way to guarantee this, yet the earthen bowl-woolen blanket method insures this also, if you work quickly and capture the heat.

Clean, grease-free utensils are most important. To quickly degrease any bowl or pot, rub the inside with a lemon cut in half. Rinse twice with warm water and allow to drip dry.

Make Yogurt Cheese

Make a light, spreadable 'pot' cheese from yogurt. It is perfect for sandwiches, spreads, dips and as a substitute for cream cheese in many instances. The cost differential is remarkable. Pot cheese is also perfect in making cheese balls and for herbed vegetable stuffings.

2 cups plain yogurt
small unbleached muslin bag, sewn with a drawstring at the top

Dampen the clean muslin (or double cheesecloth) bag with water and wring out well. Place yogurt in the bag, draw the string, and tie the bag to the sink faucet overnight to drip. The next morning remove the soft, creamy cheese and store chilled. Use generously as you would cream cheese. Makes about 1¼ cups cheese. (A pinch of sea salt will enhance this cheese just before chilling.)

Cremé Frâichê

This classic French dairy garnish is very simple to make, and is served at finer restaurants with fruits and some pastries. Consider it very fancy indeed. And very easy to make.

1 cup heavy cream, well-chilled
2 teaspoons buttermilk, commercially cultured

Combine the cream and buttermilk and heat until warmed. Remove from heat and let stand at room temperature for about 3-4 hours, or until thickened. Stir gently, then cover and chill until used.

Makes 1 cup.

Make Cream Cheese

Soft cream cheese is made with cream that is allowed to sour over time, and then is drained. This cheese is very easy, and beats the high cost of bagels and cream cheese, especially for the thick spreaders.

2 cups heavy cream

Set cream in a covered glass bowl and allow to sit at room temperature for two days. Strain through cheesecloth, then hang to drip overnight. Remove the solid cheese, chill and shape in small squares. Wrap and chill until serving. Makes about ½ pound cheese.

A Word About Whey

Whey, a by-product of the cheese-making process (curds and whey), has nutritional value which includes vitamins, minerals and protein. When making cheese, set a pan below the hanging cheesecloth and catch the dripping liquid. Chill and use in cream soups, gravies, yogurt milkshakes and other creamy foods. It is a nourishing use for this nutritious food by-product.

Make Sour Cream

Here are two ways to make sour cream at home that are so easy you'll wonder why you ever paid for it at the store!

Sour Cream: Fast

2 cups heavy cream
3 tablespoons lemon juice

Combine cream with lemon juice and let stand at room temperature for 1 hour. Cover and chill 1 hour, and use.

Makes about 1 pint.

Sour Cream: Not so Fast

2 cups heavy cream
2 tablespoons plain yogurt

Combine, cover and set in a warm place up to 8 hours or overnight. Chill, then use.

Makes about 1 pint.

Space Butter

There are a number of realities about butter like high cost, high calorie count, and cholesterol which keep many people eating alternatives which may not have butter's drawbacks but may contain artificial ingredients and in many cases milk solids nonetheless. I recommend butter over margarine whenever possible, opting for the whole food rather than the processed food. This butter spread, made with butter and cold-pressed oil, may be an answer to the butter dilemma. Keep it chilled when not in use, and substitute it in recipes measure for measure as if it were all butter.

2 cubes butter
¾ cup soy, safflower or sunflower oil

In a blender or food processor combine the butter and oil until smooth. Pour into covered containers and chill until ready for use.

Makes 1¾ cups.

Variations: For Lemony Space Butter, add ½ teaspoon lemon zest. For Herbed Space Butter add ½ teaspoon parsley and ¼ teaspoon chives together with a pinch of thyme.

Make Tofu

Tofu is a cheese curd made of soybeans. It is a highly versatile food rich in protein, minerals and vitamins while being low in calories, saturated fats and free of cholesterol. It costs half that of beef for the same amount of protein value. It is easier to digest than most other protein and is delicious in the full range of foods. And when you make it at home you have the full guarantee of freshness, plus a further savings as well. Tofu can be made from the soybeans or from soy flour. Here are both methods. When using soy flour, make sure you get a full bean flour, not a processed version. After making tofu, store immersed in water to keep it away from oxygen. When keeping tofu in your refrigerator change the water daily until you use it for maximum freshness.

Soy Flour Method: Tofu

1 level cup soy flour
4 cups water
¼ cup lemon juice
½ teaspoon sea salt

Combine the soy flour and water in a blender and whirl 4 minutes on high. Heat in a double boiler, boiling gently 20 minutes. Remove from the heat and add in the lemon juice and sea salt. Stir once, then let cool undisturbed for 30 minutes. Pour into a cheesecloth lined strainer, wrap the tofu with the cheesecloth, and allow to drip for 3 hours. For a firmer tofu, place a weight on the wrapped curd. If you want to shape the tofu, make a 5×5" wooden box with no top or bottom and press the wrapped curd into it before pressing. After firm, immerse tofu in water and store chilled until ready to cook with it.

Makes about 1 pound tofu.

Whole Bean Method: Tofu

1 cup dry soybeans
3 cups water
1½ tablespoons lemon juice

Soak the soybeans in the water overnight. Drain and rinse the beans. Add 1 cup of soaked beans plus 2 cups fresh water to the blender at a time and whirl on high for 30 seconds, or until smooth. Strain through damp cheesecloth into a saucepan. Repeat until all beans are blended and strained. Set aside the straining remains, for addition in bread or loaf entrees. Measure the strained liquid and add enough more fresh water to make 10 cups liquid. Heat gently over low heat to a boil, then remove from the heat and add in the lemon juice. Let stand 10 minutes, or until curdles form. Pour through clean cheesecloth and wrap. Place in tofu box or drain in colander. Place a weight atop the tofu for a firmer curd. Let stand at least 4 hours but as long as 12 hours (or overnight) before immersing in water and chilling. Change water every day until you use the tofu for maximum freshness.

Makes 2 cups tofu.

Make Curry Powder

Many spice combinations are simple and enduring over the centuries. Curry powder, popular in cooking from India to the Orient, is enjoying a brisk introduction in Western kitchens with delicious results from appetizers to marinated desserts. For more curry taste, increase the amount used rather than tampering with the balance of spices.

⅓ cup dark cardamon seeds, shelled
6 large cinnamon sticks
1 tablespoon whole cloves
1½ tablespoon cumin seeds
¼ teaspoon mace
¼ teaspoon nutmeg

Crush these spices together in a blender, food processor, mortar and pestle or bag with hammer until pulverized. Sift through a fairly fine mesh and discard the large pieces. Age the sifted combination in an airtight glass container for 10 days before using.

Makes about 1 cup.

Make Baking Powder

Many baking powders on the market contain alum, lime and high amounts of sodium. You can make your own baking powder, and use it measure for measure as indicated in any recipe. Your pharmacist or apothecary will be able to help you.

¼ cup potassium bicarbonate
½ cup cornstarch
½ cup cream of tartar

Combine all ingredients and sift 4 times. Store in a sealed container.

Makes 1¼ cups.

Make Kimchi

Long before Europeans pickled their first sauerkraut the various menus in Asia included a variety of cabbage condiments. In Korea it is kimchi, and no menu is considered complete without it.

2 pounds Nappa cabbage
1 pound turnips (Chinese preferred)
2 green onions
2 tablespoons ginger root, freshly ground
3 large garlic cloves
1 teaspoon red hot peppers
2 tablespoons sea salt
4 cups water
2 tablespoons sea salt
1 tablespoon honey

Clean cabbage and slice across the grain in 1" slices. Cut the turnips into ¼" thick 1" strips. Cut the onions and garlic into julienne strips. Shred the ginger root. Combine them all in a small crock. Sprinkle in the hot peppers and 2 tablespoons sea salt. Mix well with a wooden spoon and cover. Let stand at room temperature overnight. The next day combine the water, remaining salt and honey and pour over the cabbage mixture. Cover and let stand at room temperature for an additional 24 hours. Place in pint jars and refrigerate until served. Stores for 3 months. Serve as a condiment.

Makes 4 pints.

Make Sauerkraut

The virtues of fermented food are easy to obtain with sauerkraut. Fast, easy and delicious, this staple adds zing to winter dining and a finishing touch to a grilled sandwich. Make it easily:

6 pounds white cabbage
3 teaspoons coarse sea salt

Select fresh, firm juicy heads of cabbage. Clean and trim, then shred thinly. Sprinkle with the salt and place in a small crock for 30 minutes. Pound the cabbage to release the juice until the cabbage looks transparent and is covered with its own juice. Put the cabbage in a 2-3 gallon jar with a small neck and press in. Place a weight on top of the cabbage to keep it wet. Cover with a loose towel and let stand in a warm place for 3 days. Little bubbles should be coming to the surface and the liquid will be cloudy. Move to a room temperature area for about 3-5 weeks, and test weekly for the tartness you appreciate. At that time can in a hot water bath for 30 minutes.

Makes 3 quarts.

Cook with Low Energy

Low energy cooking is possible when time is not an issue, or when overnight or all-through-the-day happens to be available. Consider the thermos bottle. A cereal heated to boiling and put in a thermos overnight (lay on its side for easy extraction) will be slowly cooked and actually have more nutritional value than the cereal you struggle with first thing in the morning.

The thermos is also handy as a soup cooker. The soup you prepare in the morning and take to work in your thermos can be cooked in 4-5 hours. Try heating your raw vegetables and noodles or grains together in a broth or vegetable juice then pour into a thermos. Fresh homemade soup for lunch!

Wood stove owners can discover the advantage of slow heating breakfast cereal overnight for the morning rush, not to mention the making of stews, casseroles, soups and broths.

Earthen crocks filled with foods and heated to the boil can be wrapped in newspaper and woolen blankets and set in a warm room for the day. When evening rolls around just unwrap the crock and dinner is served, piping hot and savory from slow cooking.

Of course the crock pot, new electric invention to duplicate this method, is also available for use. And with its low consumption of energy I hope you will dust yours off and use it. If you don't own one please don't pay full price. Get yours at a garage sale instead!

Solar tea is a fast slow food. Fill a quart jar with water and two herb tea bags. Set in the sun for an hour or so. Perfectly brewed tea will result; sweet and smooth. In winter, a sunny window will do.

Food Drying

Dehydrating is considered a form of food preserving. Food drying has been done by a wood stove, in the sun or even in an oven with an over-achieving pilot light. You can make such delicious foods as raisins, dried apples, apricots, pineapple, fruit leather and jerky. Dry thin slices of tomato and zucchini as a snack with dip. Combine sprouts, fruits and vegetables and make pemmican leather for camping and hiking food. For most consistent food drying success, I suggest you investigate a food dehydrator. Offering consistent heat, air circulation and proper drying trays, these machines contribute to reliable quality results and the best use of your time, energy, effort and food dollar. For the do-it-yourselfer there are kits and directions for making a competent dehydrator. If you are serious about this preserving method it will be worthwhile to select the one best suited to your needs.

Take care, when drying foods, to slice all pieces uniformly so they dry at the same rate. Rotate the trays in your dryer from top to bottom and side to side at least once during each batch, even if the model you have guarantees "perfect" circulation. This is particularly important in damp climates. Make sure the dehydrator itself has good outside air circulation. Although they are shown as fitting right into your kitchen decor, a pantry or protected porch away from cooking odors or cramped counters will help the process.

Food drying directions are different from manufacturer to manufacturer and author to author. Each will instruct you to use methods best designed either for their machine or their personal cooking style. My slant on food drying is to use no chemicals to artificially enhance dried foods such as sulphur or lye. I recommend the use of a lemon juice bath (¼ cup per quart of lukewarm water) to hold color and moisture in foods. The vitamin C or ascorbic acid bath is

Food Drying Chart

FOOD	PREPARE	PRETREAT	DEHYDRATE	TEST
FRUITS:				
APPLE	Wash, core, (peel optional), cut in ¼" slices or rings	Vitamin C solution to hold color	115 degrees for 6-8 hours, turn over twice	Rubbery, no moisture in middle of slice
APRICOTS NECTARINES	Wash, halve, pit	1 minute blanch to remove skin (optional) Honey dip or Vitamin C dip for color	115 degrees for 36-48 hours (halves), 12 hours (slices)	Leathery, no moisture in center
BANANA	Peel and slice in round or horizontal slices, ¼" thick	Vitamin C or juice dip	125 degrees for 8 hours (turn over at 4 hours)	Crisp
BERRIES CURRANTS (FIRM)	Wash and pat dry	30 second steaming, Vitamin C dip (honey dip optional)	120 degrees for up to 12 hours (take care to rotate berries, and turn at least once	Hard and chewy
BERRIES (SOFT)	Wash, stem and gently pat dry—slice if strawberries ¼" thick	Vitamin C applied with spray bottle	115 degrees for 12 hours	Hard
CHERRIES	Wash, pit and halve	30 second steaming only if not pitted No dip	115 degrees for 12-24 hours, depending on whether whole, half and/or pitted	Chewy
FIGS	Wash, drain, pat dry —halve if large, or prick skin	30 second steam only if whole and not pricked	120 degrees for up to 48 hours if large and whole, or 12 hours for sliced	Chewy
GRAPES (RAISINS) PLUMS PRUNES	Wash, stem, slice in half and remove large seeds	If whole, unseeded then 30 second steam	115 degrees for up to 24 hours depending on size and whether whole or sliced	Chewy
LEATHERS	Wash, core, seed as needed, then blend or puree as directed	None	125 degrees for several hours depending on thickness—spread on plastic wrap to dry	Dry sticky to the touch— dry slightly longer for long storage

FOOD	PREPARE	PRETREAT	DEHYDRATE	TEST
PEACHES	Wash, halve, pit, then dry in halves or slice ¼"	Blanch 1 minute to remove skin, dip in Vitamin C or juice solution, hold in solution until ready for trays	115 degrees for 36 hours (halves), 12 hours (slices), 8 hours (chunks), turn at least twice	Leathery, no hint of moisture when bitten or cut
CITRUS PEEL	Remove white membrane, cut in ¼" thick strips	None	115 degrees for 6-8 hours	Crisp
PEARS	Peel (optional), core and slice ¼" thick	Strong Vitamin C or lemon juice dip	115 for 18 hours	Leathery, no moisture
PINEAPPLE	Skin and core, then ¼" rings, slices or pieces	None, although a honey dip will create a delicacy	115 for 24 hours	Dry and chewy
RHUBARB	Wash and cut in ½" pieces	None	115 for 8 hours	Hard
VEGETABLES:				
BEANS (STRING)	Wash and string if necessary	15-20 minute blanching	125 for 4-6 hours	Brittle
BEETS	Use small beets only, leave ½" of top	Plunge in boiling water for 30 minutes, remove skins, remove top, then cool, chop, grate or slice	120 for 8 hours	Hard slices, brittle shreds
BROCCOLI	Wash, cut in ½" pieces (skin stem and include)	Blanch 2 minutes, then drain 2 minutes—chop coarsely	120 for 12 hours Stir and rotate often	Crisp, brittle
CARROTS	Scrub, top and slice ⅛" thick	Steam 2 minutes	120 for 12 hours	Tough, but bendable
CELERY	Wash and trim stalks, slice thin (see herbs for celery leaves)	None	120 for 12 hours	Totally brittle
CORN	Husk cobs	Blanch 3 minutes, cool, cut kernels from cob	120 for 8 hours	Shriveled and dry inside

Food Drying Chart

FOOD	PREPARE	PRETREAT	DEHYDRATE	TEST
HERBS, LEAVES	Wash, pat dry	None	105—indirect air if possible	Easily crumbled
GREENS	Trim and rinse three times, pat dry	3 minute blanch	120 for 12 hours	Crisp, brittle
MUSHROOMS	Clean with damp cloth, slice ¼″	None	120 for 8 hours, stir occasionally	Tough, no moisture in center
ONIONS, GARLIC, LEEKS, SHALLOTS	Peel, ⅛″ slice or chop	None	120 for 12 hours	Brittle
PEAS	Shell fresh	3 minute blanch	120 for 12 hours	Shriveled, shatter when struck
PEPPERS, TOMATO, ZUCCHINI	Wash, remove white membrane and seeds, slice or halve	None	120 for 12 hours	Brittle
POTATO, PUMPKIN	Wash, peel, ⅛″ slices, pat starch off	8 minute steam	120 for 18 hours	Brittle
SPROUTS	Wash, drain well, pat dry	None	120 for 8 hours	Crunchy, nutty flavor

Food Dryer

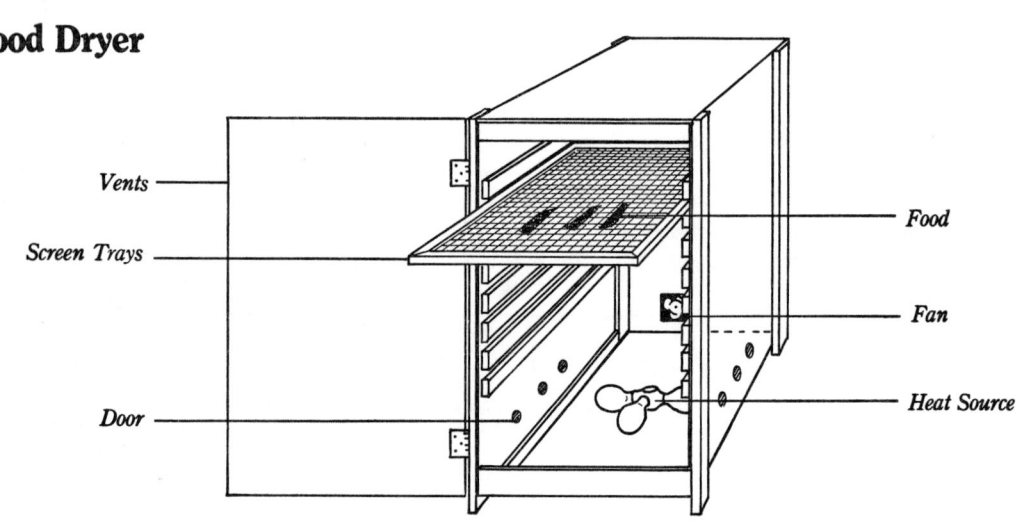

Vents
Screen Trays
Door
Food
Fan
Heat Source

28 Do It Yourself

also recommended (1 tablespoon per cup of water for easily perishable fruit like apples) (1½ teaspoons per cup of water for average dipping) for food discoloration. Buy ascorbic acid in natural food stores in crystal or powder form. I do not recommend commercial brands of this sort of product because some contain sulphur, sugar (dextrose) and other unnecessary chemicals. Straight unsweetened pineapple juice is another excellent alternative. For a special treat and a delicate effect, use the honey dip solution (1 cup honey to 1 cup water). Fruits will dry with a slightly chewy texture. This is especially tasty for fruits prepared for baking in fruit cakes. The sliced fruits will not dry as fully, but will be sticky and sweet.

Some vegetables as well as fruits will require blanching or steaming before drying. When it is called for it is necessary to halt the enzymatic action of the item. Without blanching the food will decay regardless of its moisture content. Please heed this suggestion for proper results. I do not, however, recommend any rinsing after blanching. After cooking most blanched foods will begin the dehydration step. The food drying chart will fill you in on any variations from this routine.

As with any food preserving, use only foods at their peak of freshness and condition. Fresh, unblemished foods will give the very best result. After dehydration, always test for proper drying texture. Some foods will be leathery while others must be shriveled and brittle. Some will bend while others will be crisp and crunchy. Make sure you achieve proper moisture with each food dried. Cut with a knife or bite through a leathery item to make sure it is dry clear through. Strike a pea or corn kernel to assure that it shatters.

To store dried foods, first seal in a plastic storage bag, then place in glass jars with tight fitting lids. Watch for beading moisture for the next few days. If moisture appears, redry the foods involved or they will mold and perish. Also be on the lookout for insects. Store all packaged foods in a dry, cool place out of direct sunlight. Dried foods will last many years if necessary, but eat them within a year for peak taste.

To reconstitute foods for eating, place the item in a glass bowl and just cover with boiling water. Let stand several hours or until all the water is absorbed. Test by tasting if the item has gained full moisture or may require a bit more. For faster results, place item in a saucepan and cover with boiling water. Simmer 20 minutes, or until most of the water is absorbed. Let stand, covered for another 20 minutes, then test for use. In either case, include any accompanying liquid in your dish, as it contains the essence of the food involved.

The food drying chart offers direction for commonly dehydrated foods. It describes how to prepare, pretreat (when necessary), dry and test the food involved. If you want to dry a food not listed, choose the directions for the food family closest resembling the food you have. Make a small test batch to check for procedure suitability.

The chart is made for a slow, temperature-regulated, fan-circulating dehydrator similar to one which would be made at home. Compare the drying times suggested for your machine if it is more sophisticated. Note also that batch volume will affect drying time, so work with the machine and find your own level with it. Climate humidity will also affect the time, as will fruit ripeness as well as thickness. Remember to turn your foods over at least once during processing, and to rotate trays. Further, combining certain foods together for simultaneous drying may not be advisable (onions-bananas). Common sense rules here.

Red Meat Jerky

Beef, lamb, pork, game and poultry can be successfully dried for jerky. It is important to trim all excess fat from your meat and slice uniformly at ¼" thick or less. Cure meat first in either a salt and water brine with other seasonings included (as with a marinade) or use the dry curing method, which involves applying salt and seasonings directly to the meat. (I suggest rejecting nitrates in jerky making, since they are unnecessary and also require perfect temperature control.) After your meat has cured overnight, dry at 140 degrees for the first 4 hours, then reduce the heat to 130 for another 4 hours. Blot oil beads from the surface of the meat from time to time, and remember to rotate and turn the jerky at least once during the process. Jerky is done if, when cool, it cracks when bent and has no wet spots.

Beef Jerky Marinade

4 pounds lean meat (chuck or round)
½ cup Worcestershire sauce
½ cup soy sauce
2 tablespoons tomato sauce
2 tablespoons white vinegar
1 teaspoon honey
½ teaspoon garlic powder
½ teaspoon onion powder
2 teaspoons salt
1 teaspoon red wine

Have meat sliced by your butcher or freeze the meat until firm and slice across the grain at ¼" or less. Combine the remaining ingredients in a blender and whirl 2 minutes. Arrange the meat 1 layer thick in shallow pans and pour marinade over all. Refrigerate overnight and dry.

Fish Drying

Clean and dress the fish of your choice. Slice into strips about ¼" thick. Prepare a brine of ½ cup salt to 1 quart water. Soak fish for 30 minutes. Rinse, then place them on a clean flat surface. Liberally sprinkle each fish strip with a dry cure mixture (see below), using about 1 tablespoon cure for every 2 pounds of fish involved. Place seasoned fish in an airtight container and refrigerate 8 hours. Rotate the container at least once during this time. Dry the fish strips in the dehydrator at 150 degrees for 12 hours, or until dry. Rotate and turn once during this time. Fish jerky will be done when firm, dry and tough. It will not crumble and there should be no moist spots. Store in airtight containers. It will last 3 months at room temperature, or 6 months frozen.

Gourmet Dry Cure

4 pounds fish
2 tablespoons salt
1 teaspoon celery salt
¼ cup parsley flakes, crushed
1 bay leaf, crushed
1 teaspoon black pepper, freshly ground
¼ teaspoon thyme
1 teaspoon onion powder
3 tablespoons dry white wine

Slice fish at ¼". Combine next 7 ingredients in a blender and pulverize. Sprinkle over fish, then pour wine evenly over all. Refrigerate 8 hours then dry as directed.

Cooking with a Food Processor

Kitchen-sized food processors are finally making their way into homes. Now that I have one I wonder why I put it off. It is perfect for making bread (yes, even whole grain dough, although the direction books decline whole grain recipes), pie dough (I discovered my aversion to making pie was the hassle of the dough. Now pie, quiche and other pastry foods are easier and lots faster!), dips, spreads, fruit smoothies, leftover soup (you know, stock plus all the vegetables in the refrigerator plus a little milk), cookies, pizza ingredients and tons of other foods that you only dreamed of making because the ingredients required finely ground this or creamy smooth that.

If you need to rationalize your purchase as a formal budget request of family funds there are two ways to do it. The easiest is that "time is money" and a food processor in the kitchen is like having a cooperative assistant. Your food preparation time is greatly reduced. Also significantly worth mentioning is the ability to turn leftovers into magnificent meals and save all sorts of money serving delicious food in unrecognizable yet delectable new ways. Just the other day I recycled 4 small hunks of cheese that had dried and gone to heaven, a dab of corn, a dab of buttermilk and sour cream and some leftover potatoes into perfect au gratin potatoes. Four minutes preparation time and it did taste like I'd worked all afternoon.

When venturing into creative cooking or using whole foods, keep these tips in mind: refer back to your manual for the order of foods when making a recipe similar to one in your manual. Order is very important with these machines. Large stuff first, smaller second. For pureeing, use no liquid. Only the puree victim is necessary. When creaming butter with honey, drizzle the honey in. Then the eggs, then the flour. (With sugar, the eggs and sugar are first, then the butter.)

A food processor is not designed for whipping. Mashing potatoes, whipping cream or egg whites or other items requiring air will not be satisfactory. The blade motion is not designed for this.

The food processor is designed for slicing, cutting, shredding and blending. It will make a smooth mixture very fast. Most items which start out lumpy or coarse will benefit from the "pulse" motion of the blade. This allows for the ingredients to settle back down on the blade and will actually get the job of mixing done faster than continued motion. Long-term mixing, on the other hand, will benefit from the continuous motion of the blade.

From guacamole to veggie dippers and pâté to pastry dough, it would be hard to go back to manual labor after knowing the joys of an extra hand in the kitchen. And the fine quality of the results will make that return a primitive one. I'll keep mine, and use it every chance I get.

Terminology

Whole Wheat Flour—an excellent food, containing more than 28 naturally occuring vitamins and minerals. The wheat berry contains three major sections: endosperm (starchy center with a small portion of protein), bran (large amounts of vitamins, minerals and protein), and wheat germ (rich in B vitamins and vitamin E, plus protein and unsaturated fatty acids). When wheat is "stone-ground", a low temperature method of grinding, it offers the full complement of nutritional value. Instead of sifting your flour before measuring, try fluffing it with a fork. This will guard against heavy measuring, and will save larger bran flakes for the goodness of the recipe. For substituting whole grain flour into a "white flour recipe", use 1⅞ cups whole wheat flour for every 2 cups of white flour called for. Generally, whole wheat flour is used in recipes which require yeast-raising or a hearty texture. It is high in gluten, the elastic quality which creates breads that rise properly. To insure freshness, use any whole wheat flour you purchase within 60 days. Store in a cool, dry place. Flour may be stored in the freezer, double-wrapped if you prefer.

Whole Wheat Pastry Flour—the perfect flour for quick breads, light pastries and cookies. This flour is made from the kernels of a different variety of wheat, and is lower in gluten. The basic nutritional benefits of the 'soft white wheat' are the same as for the whole wheat flour used in yeast breadmaking. The storage techniques and substitution ratios are the same also. This flour is found most commonly in pasta making, pie crust, cookies, cakes, pancakes and crepes and offers a light and flaky product. It is also appropriate for gravy thickening and fish or chicken dredging. When using baking powder or soda, this is the flour of choice.

Unbleached Flour—milled endosperm of the whole grain, this flour is starchy and contains marginal nutritional value. It does not, however, contain extra bromides used for processing bleached (chemically colored and aged) flour. Our culture has become used to eating its bread products "white", so for the recipe that just can't be tampered with, unbleached flour is the preferred alternative. To improve the nutritional value of unbleached flour without altering the color of the end product, include 1 tablespoon soy flour in every cup of unbleached flour used. Wean your family and yourself from unbleached flour gradually by slow substitutions of whole grain flours into recipes. Over time, your tastebuds will adjust to the more flavorful combination and your preference will grow.

Whole Grain Flours—flours of all grains are available and add nutritious alternatives to the diet. **Graham Flour** is simply coarse whole wheat flour. When hard to find, add 1 tablespoon bran to each cup whole wheat flour for a reasonable substitute. **Corn meal** and **corn flour** are magnificent when fresh and make memorable occasions of the foods they are in. **Oat flour, rye flour** and **rye meal** (coarse rye flour), **rice flour** (white, brown and high gluten or mochi all have their own uses), **potato flour, soy flour** and **barley flour** are also available and have their special uses among baking. Select these flours carefully since their use is not as common and stock turnover may lag. Buy bulk whenever possible and judge freshness by smell. Flour which smells sweet and hearty, or which has no smell at all is considered edible. Flour which has a rancid, sour or flat smell is not fresh. Dont buy it. Most grain flours listed here are not high in gluten and do not respond to yeast-rising without help.

Eighty Percent Gluten Flour (Do Pep)—a highly concentrated flour additive, used to add gluten to low gluten flours for the purpose of obtaining a yeast-rising bread. This product works well and will give success with rye flour, oat, barley and others. Use ¼ cup Do-Pep for every 2 cups of low-gluten flour in the recipe. Combine the Do-Pep with the flour before adding to wet ingredients, due to the lumping quality of the Do-Pep. It is also successful in improving the quality of low-protein unbleached flour, poor quality whole wheat flour, or grainy graham flour. Use 1 tablespoon per cup of these flours in the recipe. Again, mix in before adding. Do not be tempted to use more than suggested here. It will not work miracles on garbage flour. It will, however, turn garbage flour into very useful door stops or paper weights. No doubt the highest use possible under the circumstances, yet a sad waste of the other ingredients.

Whole Grains—the use of unprocessed grains in all areas of eating is encouraged. Whole grains are added to baking, simmered and served for breakfast, sprouted, steamed, cracked and baked. To prepare grains, wash in cold water once or twice. Saute 1 cup grain in 2 tablespoons safflower oil until browned. Add in 2 cups water, cover and steam until tender. Steaming time will vary with the grain involved, and sauteing decreases the total simmering time involved. Rather than steaming, put sauteed grains, covered into a 350° oven along with other dinner items and bake 1 hour. To release full nutritional value from grains, soak overnight in the water you intend to cook the grains in. Simmer until tender. Optimally, cook grains overnight in a crockpot or thermos bottle. Long, low heat doubles the nutritional value of whole grains, the most popular of which are brown rice, oats, barley, rye, millet, buckwheat, wheat, triticale, soy and corn.

Bran and Germ—the outer covering of grain, and the embryo or new life of the grain. These two items are results of processed flour manufacturing. Bran is rich in vitamins, minerals and proteins. It is also famed for its high natural roughage or cellulose content which encourages timely intestinal functioning. Germ contains valuable unsaturated fatty acids and vitamin E, essential to cardiovascular strength. The two most common brans and germs are from wheat and corn. Both are available and have high dietary value. When whole grain wheat or corn are not available, you can "re-invent" them by adding 1 tablespoon bran and germ for every two cups flour involved. Wheat germ is also an interesting ingredient to substitute for part of the flour in a quick bread recipe such as brownies. An intense food, it contributes to a delicious breakfast when combined with plain yogurt, walnuts and honey.

Sea Salt—mined from the sea, it contains trace minerals and elements not found in earth-mined salts. Sea salt generally avoids the non-lumping chemicals added to earth salt also. (Use brown rice in your shaker instead!) Use slightly less sea salt in a recipe. All salt is high in sodium, however, including sea salt. I suggest that decreased salt consumption is advisable. In general cooking, reduce all salt by ½ or more. Yeast baking requires salt however, so be careful when reducing sea salt here. Never take out more than ½, since the yeast/salt balance is critical for rising. (Do not adjust the salt in this book, as it is already adjusted! Of course.)

Kelp—seaweed, high in minerals and iodine, which gives a salt flavor to food with only 1/16th the sodium. Kelp is an excellent regulator of the body, offering advantages for the weight-watcher as well as the dull of skin. An all-around seasoning, kelp powder is perfect as a salt substitute in cooking. It sprinkles out of any container with slightly enlarged holes. It is available in bulk as well as commercial dispensers. Begin to eliminate your heavy use of salt in cooking by using kelp powder at the stove. Have salt only at the table for last minute additions to such foods as popcorn or fresh radishes. This simple cooking adjustment will eliminate about half your family's salt consumption almost immediately. Don't let the dark green color of the kelp powder discourage you. It cooks into foods easily and vanishes. When eliminating salt from yeast-rising breads, only substitute about 1/3 kelp powder for the salt required. Yeast requires salt to ferment properly. Also note that the recipes in this book have already been adjusted.

Cold-Pressed Oils—oils extracted by pressing rather than with the aid of a chemical catalyst or high heat, or both. Safflower oil, soy oil, sunflower oil and peanut oil are the most common of these oils. They may be slightly darker in color or heartier in flavor, yet the method of extraction excludes chemical residue or saturated fats from your table. Peanut oil has the highest temperature resistance and is preferred for deep-frying. Safflower oil has the lightest taste and is preferred for salad dressings. Soy oil and sunflower oil are high in complete nutritional value and may be your choice for general cooking. I keep several around, and even mix them from time to time when all the bottles get low. Tip for Sauteing: when sauteing with butter, add in a teaspoon of oil for every 2 tablespoons of butter used. It will prevent the butter from burning and splattering and allow sauteing to continue for a longer period of time.

Dairy Products—fresh, unprocessed dairy foods and dairy foods prepared without the use of non-essential ingredients (such as sugar, starch and synthetic vitamins) are preferred. Raw milk products are available in some areas, and generally are state-regulated and safe. Use natural, unprocessed dairy foods whenever possible. Butter is a prime example, and is superior to powdered-milk-fortified margarines. Natural yogurt, undyed cheese, naturally cultured milks and naturally flavored ice creams and frozen desserts are a few more reasons to eat food, not chemicals. Select foods made with whole, unprocessed, undyed, real ingredients.

Milk Powder—non-instant milk powder is recommended for its higher nutritional value. Available as non-fat and buttermilk powders, it is perfect for yogurt-making, cheese-making and recipe inclusion not only as the milk called for, but as an additional protein booster. It is also used to make frostings because of its similar consistency to powdered sugar, and its sweet taste. Avoid "instantized" or over-processed milk powder.

Blackstrap Molasses—a by-product of the sugar making process, blackstrap molasses carries with it high concentrations of iron and B vitamins which are in the initial sugar mash before processing. Unsulphured molasses is made without catalyst and will be sweeter, less bitter and free of chemical residues. Molasses may be substituted for honey measure for measure, or in combination depending upon your taste. As a spring tonic and dietary supplement, 1 teaspoon in a glass of warm water daily will add an extra measure of nutrition to your menu.

Raw Honey—honey extracted from the comb without the use of high heat. Honey is a natural, unprocessed alternative to processed sugar, and I highly recommend it. While sugar is a refined, processed carbohydrate, honey stands alone as a natural food, unprocessed and offering enzymes and unrefined carbohydrates for the body. Though honey is not a diet food, it is a real food, involving the body in its metabolism. Avoid processed sugar products at all times and substitute raw honey. To do this, for every cup of sugar required in a recipe, use ½ cup honey, and remove ¼ cup of another liquid in the recipe. When using honey, beat it briskly into the butter or oil called for to give it fluffiness and body. Dumping honey into a recipe will cause a heavy result when baking. Whip lightly before proceeding and success will follow. Be aware that not all honey is the same. Avoid really thin honey or white, fluffy honey. You may be buying extra water with the first and extra air with the second. Stick with thicker, slightly cloudy honey, preferably from a local apiary (bee farmer) you know. Ask where the hives are placed and avoid federal lands or crops which have been sprayed. The bees will pass the chemicals on to you. Bee pollen, also manufactured by bees, is a highly concentrated food high in protein and enzymes. It is used for colds, and also by runners and other athletes for carbohydrate loading and for extra energy when a meal is not advisable. It is delicious when chewed and is best eaten raw.

Farm Fresh Eggs—white eggs and brown eggs are of equal nutritional value, as long as they come from the same farm. The old city myth favoring brown eggs is true only when the chickens involved are allowed to run free, scratch for their food and live and lay their eggs by the dictates of the sun and the moon. Egg nutrition flags when the birds are force-fed, cooped up and force-stimulated to live 16-hour days. In 18 months the chickens are burnt-out and are sent (you guessed it) to slaughter. Make every effort to purchase "free-run" eggs.

Carob—an excellent substitute for chocolate in all cooking, carob contains none of the fat and half the calories of chocolate. Carob is high in natural sweetener while chocolate requires sugar for flavor development. Carob has no caffeine or theobromine, which is found in chocolate, and people with chocolate allergy can generally eat carob without an allergic reaction. In addition, carob is high in vitamins and minerals while chocolate is sadly low in nutritive value. To substitute carob in a recipe, use 3 tablespoons carob powder plus 2 tablespoons water for every one ounce square of chocolate. If using cocoa powder, substitute measure for measure. When using carob powder, sift before adding to other dry ingredients to avoid lumps. Always mix with other dry ingredients before adding to wet ingredients, since lumping here is a problem also. Generally, also add a dash of cloves and a double measure of vanilla to enhance the carob flavor to its fullest potential. Carob is also known by other names. St. John's Bread is the most common. Untoasted carob pods are often found as tamarind seeds, from which a sweet Caribbean beverage is made. The carob or tamarind pod, untoasted, is a common natural treat, used by the children of Europe during the war as candy. Easy carob syrup for banana splits is made by combining 1 tablespoon carob powder, ½ cup honey and 1 tablespoon butter over a double boiler and heating until thick and bubbly. Add a dash of cloves and ¼ teaspoon vanilla and whisk until smooth. Pour over ice cream to serve.

Herb Teas—delicious, healthful beverages made from leaves, roots, flowers and twigs of edible plants. The proper brewing of herb tea is easy, yet important. Sweet, delicate herbs prepared properly do not require extra sweetening. One teabag of herb tea or 1 teaspoon of bulk tea is placed into 1 cup water which has to come to a boil. The pot is covered, removed from the heat and allowed to sit, or steep, for 3-5 minutes. The resulting liquid is strained and served in a mug or tea cup. Depending upon your taste, the tea may be stronger or weaker by subtracting or adding water at this time. For larger batches of tea, 1 bag for every two cups is sufficient. Herb tea is also excellent iced, and frozen herb tea makes an excellent base for refreshing punch or a perfect ice mold for the center of a punch bowl.

APPETIZERS
Beverages and Condiments

Easy Spring Rolls

The joy of hot egg rolls without the deep frying.

½ cup celery, minced
¼ cup onion, minced
1 tablespoon green onion, finely minced
½ cup water chestnuts, chopped
¼ cup bamboo shoots, chopped
⅔ cup bean sprouts, loosely cut
¾ cup shrimp, washed and drained
1 teaspoon soy sauce
2 tablespoons cornstarch
½ cup safflower oil
12 sheets filo dough

Steam the celery, onion, green onion and water chestnuts over rapidly boiling water until the celery is tender. Remove and combine with the bamboo shoots, bean sprouts and shrimp. Toss lightly, then sprinkle in the soy sauce and cornstarch. Blend well until the mixture becomes slightly thickened. With a wide pastry brush paint a filo dough sheet with oil. Place another sheet on top and repeat. Place the third sheet on top, then place about ¼ of the vegetable mixture at one end of the dough, in a line. Roll and tuck the dough to the end. Repeat until the dough and vegetable mixture are used. Place the rolls, seam down on an unoiled baking sheet. Bake at 375 for about 15 minutes. Serve, cut in 1½" slices. Serve with hot Chinese mustard and soy sauce to garnish.

Makes about 24 slices.

Handy Hint: Save crumbs and seeds from the bottom of bread bags and use as bread crumbs.

Oysters Nevalle

For oyster lovers everywhere (we know who we are) and for all those wonderful people who give me their share too.

16 ounces oysters, drained (use small size)
¼ cup dry vermouth
¼ cup lemon juice
2 tablespoons lime juice
5 tablespoons butter, melted
pepper to taste
3 tablespoons parsley, finely minced

Place oysters in a lightly oiled baking dish, one layer deep and bake at 300 for about 20 minutes. Whisk together the fruit juices, vermouth and butter, then pour over the baked oysters. Brown them under the broiler for about 3-4 minutes, then garnish with fresh pepper and parsley. Serve them on a platter with toothpicks, and a little dish of the rendered juices from the baking dish.

Makes about 20-24.

Karly's Guac Sticks

High in the Amador County wine country of Northern California the Karly Winery produces fine wine. And the vintner's kitchen keeps that tradition alive, serving foods to their special guests with a sublime elegance unmatched. An early evening appetizer that is favored among guests is the guac stick, a portable tortilla filled with guacamole.

2 ripe avocados
juice of ¼ lemon
1 teaspoon onion, minced
8 large flour tortillas

Combine the avocado flesh, lemon juice and onion with a fork or in a food processor, and mash until almost smooth. Heat the tortillas on a dry skillet until warmed but not hot. Spread the guacamole evenly among the tortillas (about 2 tablespoons each), then roll and finally finish the end like an envelope. Eat immediately.

Serves 8 sticks. Usually to 4 people.

Taco Pyramid

There is a quiet contest brewing among the lounges, restaurants and kitchens of this land to see who can "out-Nacho" whom. It started with corn chips, then quickly spread to cheese-covered tortilla chips. From there it progressed to cheese-drenched, guacamole covered, sour cream dolloped and black olive bespeckled melted all over 'real' tortilla chips. My taco pyramid may not stop the show, but it will surely slow you down until they think of something else to put on top.

1 cup taco sauce
¼ cup green chiles, minced
1 cup mushrooms, sliced
1 cup fresh tomatoes, chopped
1 avocado
1 tablespoon lemon juice
2 cups cheddar cheese, shredded
¾ cup black olives, coarsely sliced
½ cup sour cream
2 family-size bags tortilla chips

In a small saucepan, simmer together the taco sauce, chiles, mushrooms and fresh tomatoes for 5 minutes. Set aside. Mash the avocado flesh with a fork, adding in the lemon juice to blend well. On a very large platter spread the tortilla chips about 2 chips deep. Sprinkle the cheese over the chips and put under the broiler until melted. Pour hot sauce over the toasted chips, then cover with the guacamole. Garnish with the black olives and sour cream and serve immediately. Judge whether you want to make one large serving or two smaller servings, and divide the ingredients accordingly. Either way, this appetizer will keep them happy for quite a while.

Serves about 8 people.

Beer-Batter Onion Rings

If you are like me, the whole meal could be onion rings. This simple recipe takes the worry out of breathing close, since no one will resist the light, crunchy zest they offer.

1½ cups beer, room temperature
1½ cups whole wheat pastry flour
3 large yellow onions
peanut oil for frying

Combine the flour and the beer with a wire whisk and whip until smooth. Cover the bowl and let sit at room temperature for at least 3 hours. Preheat your oven to 200 degrees. Cut your onions in ¼" rings. Heat the peanut oil to about 375 degrees, and have 2-2½" of oil in your pan. Dip a few onions into the batter, then fry. When golden crisp keep them warm in the oven while continuing the process. Serve hot.

Note: Long cooking chopsticks are very handy when turning the onion rings, and tend to keep you farther away from the hot oil.

Serves 8.

Shrimp Won Ton

This hot hors d'oeuvre is a favorite world-over. Perfect for patio or around a cozy fire.

½ pound shrimp, chopped and patted dry
¼ cup onion, diced
¼ cup crab, chopped and patted dry
¼ cup bamboo shoots, sliced
¼ cup bean sprouts, chopped
3 tablespoons green onion, minced
1 teaspoon vegetable salt
1 teaspoon soy sauce
1 tablespoon cornstarch
12-ounce package won ton wrappers, fresh or thawed
1 egg white, lighty whisked
enough peanut oil to fry 2" deep

In a medium bowl toss together the meats and vegetables. Sprinkle on the seasonings and cornstarch and mix well. Fill each won ton wrapper with 1 teaspoon of filling. Seal the two joining sides of the wrapper with egg white, then fold as shown. Fry in deep oil for three minutes at 375 degrees, turning occasionally until golden brown. Drain on paper towel for just a minute, then serve.

Note: If won ton wrappers are not available, use filo dough instead. Seal three layers of filo together with egg white, then cut into 3" square pieces. Proceed as above.

Makes about 36.

1. Fill wrapper.   *2. Apply egg white.*

 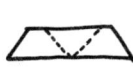 

3. Fold.

Hot, Tropical Cheese Delights

1 cup cottage cheese
¾ cup tofu (may substitute feta)
½ cup cream cheese
1 egg
⅔ cup pineapple, drained and crushed
2 teaspoons chives, minced
1 tablespoon parsley, minced
½ cup safflower oil
12 sheets filo dough

Cream the cheeses and tofu together, then include the egg and whip until very smooth. Add in the pineapple and seasonings and blend thoroughly. With a wide pastry brush paint oil on a filo sheet, then lay another sheet on top. Paint it with the oil also, then lay a third sheet on that. Place about ½" wide strip of filling along one side of the dough, and roll and tuck it until the log is finished. Do this until the filo dough and batter are used. Place these logs, seal down on an unoiled baking sheet. Bake at 375° for about 15 minutes. Remove and cool, then slice in 1½" pieces. Serve immediately.

Makes about 24 hot morsels.

Summer Toothpick Salad

Get around the formal sit-down salad course with this great way to refresh the palate.

2 cups cantaloupe balls
2 cups honeydew melon balls
2 ripe pears, chunked
4 rings pineapple, quartered
1 firm avocado, crescent-cut
6 tablespoons safflower oil
2 tablespoons apple cider vinegar
1 teaspoon parsley, minced
1 teaspoon chives, minced
1 mint leaf, minced
pepper to taste

Prepare all fruits as suggested and arrange in deep bowl. In a smaller bowl, whisk together the oil, vinegar and fresh herbs. Grind in a little pepper to taste. Pour the dressing over the salad mixture and toss lightly. Cover and chill up to three hours, tossing lightly every hour. Serve with toothpicks, arranging salad on a lettuce-covered platter.

Serves 8.

Heavenly Hommus

When hommus combines with whole grain bread and vegetables it provides a high protein food. This mixture is suitable as a dip for vegetables, a dip for bread and also as a sandwich spread with or without accompaniment. And the tangy flavor keeps them coming back for more.

15 oz. can garbanzo beans, reserve juice
¼ cup sesame tahini
1 tablespoon olive oil
juice of ½ lemon
2 medium garlic cloves
½ teaspoon soy sauce
pepper to taste

In a blender, food processor or mixing bowl, mix together the garbanzo beans, sesame tahini and olive oil until very smooth. Add in lemon juice, garlic cloves and seasonings, then slowly add in the reserved liquid until hommus is the consistency of thin frosting (which is still spreadable.) Chill, covered for about an hour. Garnish with parsley sprig and serve.

Serving suggestion: This dish is most effectively served in combination with sliced vegetables and flat cracker bread or pocketbread. To complete the course, a hearty rose or sparkling strawberry-apple spritzer will do nicely.

Makes about 1½ cups.

Handy Hint: Crisp lettuce, spinach and other salad greens. When first home from the store, wash greens and wrap in cloth toweling. Store in plastic bag until ready to use. Greens will be more crisp and will hold dressing better.

Vegetable-Shrimp Dip

The perfect dip for a platter of vegies.

1 cup zucchini, shredded
1 cup undyed cheddar cheese, shredded
1 cup shrimp, drained and chopped
½ cup walnuts, chopped
¾ cup plain yogurt
½ cup mayonnaise
1 tablespoon parsley, chopped
1 teaspoon chives, minced

Toss together the zucchini, cheese, shrimp and walnuts. Spoon the yogurt and mayonnaise on top and whip vigorously. Sprinkle on the herbs and whip again. Chill 1 hour before serving. Garnish with a dash of paprika. Arrange various vegetables on a platter and serve with it.

Note: For a smaller party, cut this recipe in half. It is also good as a sandwich spread or club sandwich filling.

Makes 4 cups.

Tuxedo Crab Spread

The delicate taste of crab is elegantly complimented in this spread. Serve with crisp melba, whole grain pretzels or strong tortilla chips for an extra treat.

1 pound crab, chopped and patted dry
2 hard-boiled eggs, finely minced
½ cup Gruyere cheese, shredded
1 green onion, finely minced
juice of 1 lemon
½ cup mayonnaise (adjust for moistness)
¼ teaspoon curry powder

Toss the crab, eggs, cheese and onion together until combined. Sprinkle on the lemon juice. Add in the mayonnaise and curry powder and mix until smooth. Chill 1 hour, covered. Serve with crackers. Keeps well for 2-3 days.

Note: This is a perfect item that can be made ahead. If you can stay out of it until your guests come!

Makes about 2½ cups of spread.

Don't Change It Dip

When first experimenting with my new food processor, I happened to have an abundance of all sorts of ingredients in the refrigerator and thought of making a fast dip to keep the troops quiet while I made dinner one particularly late evening. This terrific dip (which may also be made in a blender or with an electric mixer), is the result.

4 ounces cream cheese
½ cup ricotta
¾ cup cottage cheese
½ cup plain yogurt
3 tablespoons lemon juice
1 green onion
1 tablespoon vegetable salt
2 teaspoons soy sauce

Place all ingredients into the bowl of the machine of your choice and whip until smooth. Serve with chips, pita bread, fresh-cut vegetables or apples.

Makes 2½ cups dip.

David's Add-A-Dabba Dip

After the rush of the new year was over and the task of returning the contents of the refrigerator to its normal, boring fare, my youngest fledgling chef found a selection of dabs of ingredients and decided to turn them into a dip for the poor, unfortunate bag of chips also left in the cupboard.

½ cup jalapeno cheddar cheese
½ cup sour cream
⅓ cup cottage cheese
⅓ cup Parmesan cheese
1 sweet pickle

Combine all ingredients together in a food processor or blender and whip until smooth. Taste to make sure the Parmesan is about half its original grittiness. Chill for 2 hours before serving. Serve with chips, vegetables and crackers.

Makes 1¾ cups dip.

Sweet Berry Wine Punch

1 lemon grass herb tea bag
1 rosehip herb tea bag
4 cups water
1 cup fresh strawberries or raspberries
1 quart strawberry-apple juice
4/5 quart of berry wine
1 lime

Brew the herb teas in the water for 5 minutes, then cool completely. Place the fresh berries in ice cube trays and cover with the tea. Freeze until hard. When ready to serve the punch, empty the ice cubes into a 1 gallon punch bowl and pour the fruit juice and wine over the ice cubes. Slice the lime into very thin circles and garnish the punch.

The beauty of this recipe is the number of variations that are possible. Various fruit juice combinations together with bright wines and tasty herbal ice cubes will keep you refreshed all year long. Using the above ratios, try the following combinations for excellent sipping:
—hibiscus herb tea, pomegranate juice, white wine
—Lemon grass herb tea, pineapple slices, pineapple-coconut juice, sparkling water
—rose hip herb tea, raisins, cranberry-apple juice, rose wine

Serves 24 4-ounce glasses.

Classic Papaya Smoothie

Best memories of Hawaii always include at least a daily fruit smoothie. And this is my favorite.

½ ripe papaya, pared, seeded and chopped
4 strawberries
¼ cup coconut milk
1 cup plain yogurt
½ cup milk
juice of ½ lime
1 egg
3 ice cubes

Place everything in the blender together and whip until completely smooth, about 2 minutes. Serve in iced glasses.

Serves 3 8-ounce glasses.

The Grand O.J.

This smooth and elegant evening beverage is perfect around the fire. Definitely a dress-up drink.

2½ cups orange juice, chilled
1 cup plain yogurt
½ cup Grand Marnier
  (any cognac will almost do)
nutmeg to garnish

In the blender whip together the orange juice and plain yogurt. Slowly drizzle in the liqueur until all is blended well. Pour into a chilled pitcher and garnish with fresh nutmeg.

Serves 8 4-ounce glasses. (Realistically, four guests will polish this off quickly.)

Variation: To turn this into a lighter beverage, simply include 2 cups sparkling water after blending. Swizzle briskly and serve.

Serves 12 4-ounce glasses.

Vegetarian Frappe

Combining my favorite vegetables into a vegetable cocktail any bartender would get rich on!

1½ cups fresh carrot juice
1½ cups tomato juice
½ cup cucumber, pared, seeded and chopped
1 tablespoon green pepper, chopped
2 drops Tabasco sauce
1 cup sparkling water
parsley sprigs to garnish
6 celery sticks to garnish

In the blender whip together the carrot and tomato juices along with the cucumber and green pepper. When smooth, slowly add in the Tabasco sauce and sparkling water. Pour into tumblers over ice and garnish with parsley and celery stalks.

Makes 6 amazing drinks for 6 equally amazed guests.

Avocumber Dilly Delight

Go Green! This delightful vegetable smoothie really hits the spot. It will serve equally well as a summer cooler or as a unique salad course to a patio party. It can even double as the soup course, served in chilled bowls.

½ cup cucumber, pared, seeded and chopped
1 medium avocado, pared, pitted and chopped
1 green onion, minced
2 tablespoons lemon juice
2½ cups milk
1 cup plain yogurt
1 teaspoon dill weed
dash garlic powder
dash white pepper

In a large blender or food processor combine the cucumber, avocado, green onion and lemon juice until smooth. Mix in the milk, yogurt and seasonings and chill briefly. Garnish with fresh parsley sprig and lemon wedge if you wish.

Serves about 6 7-ounce servings.

Hard Cider Cocktail

Warm, cozy, delicious.

1 gallon hard apple cider
6 cups apple wine (economy brand)
juice of 1 lemon
juice of 1 orange
1 orange decorated with cloves
2 cinnamon sticks, broken
3 tablespoons raw honey

Combine the cider and wine in a 2 gallon electric coffee maker. Add in the lemon and orange juices, then add in the decorated orange, the cinnamon sticks and the honey. Stir with a chopstick or other suitable long implement. Heat and serve.

Makes about 30 6-ounce servings.

Watermelon Chablis Spritzer

2 cups watermelon balls
½ cup Chablis or any light white wine
24 ounces sparkling water
up to ¾ cup watermelon juice
6 mint leaf sprigs.

Place the watermelon balls in a shallow dish and marinate with the Chablis for 3 hours. Spoon the balls into 8 champagne glasses. Combine the remaining wine together with the sparkling water and rendered watermelon juice. Stir quickly, then pour over the watermelon balls in the glasses. Garnish with mint sprigs and serve.

Note: This beverage is so special that it may even be served as a dessert course to a heavier meal.

Serves 8.

Heather's Graduation Punch

This light, refreshing punch is perfect for large crowds as well as small groups. The taste is crisp and the ice cubes are the secret.

2 peppermint herb tea bags
4 cups water
4/5 quart of carbonated apple juice
4/5 quart of peach wine or fruity white wine
1 lemon

Brew the tea bags in the boiling water for 5 minutes. Cool slightly, then freeze in ice cube trays until hard. Place frozen ice cubes in 1 gallon punch bowl, then pour the carbonated apple juice and peach wine over them. Slice the lemon into very thin slices, and garnish the punch. Stir once, then serve.

Serves about 20 people a wine glassful (4-6 ounces.)

Naughty Nectarine Smoothie

3 ripe nectarines, pitted and chopped
1 very ripe banana, peeled and sliced
1 cup plain yogurt
1½ cups milk
few drops vanilla
4 ice cubes
1 shot Brandy (optional)

Puree the banana and nectarines together in the blender. Add in the yogurt, milk, ice cubes and vanilla and whip 2 minutes, or until ice is dissolved into the mixture. Continue to whip, adding in the Brandy very slowly, until all is included. Serve in chilled tumblers.

Serves 5.

Apricot Vinegar

Renewed interest in vinegars that are flavored with herbs has also revived an interest in fruited vinegars. They are used when making a slightly sweet salad dressing, or when the hint of a fruit flavor is the perfect accent to the ingredients involved.

2 pounds fresh apricots, pitted (reserve pits)
2 cups apple cider vinegar

Chop the fruit very fine, then mash well. Pour the vinegar over the mashed fruit. Remove the nut from 3 apricot pits and include them in the mixture. Stir the mixture briefly and let it stand in a cool place for 2 days. Cover loosely with cheesecloth or wire mesh, and do not disturb. Strain the aged apricot mixture through a jelly bag or tripled cheesecloth. Discard the pulp and pits. Fill ½ pint jars and seal. Process in a hot water bath for 15 minutes at a boil.

Variation: Other fruits are also suited to this process. Peaches, nectarines and plums are excellent, as well as sweet cherries. The directions are the same in all cases.

Makes 4-5 ½ pint jars fruited vinegar.

Handy Hint: Before whipping cream, place the metal whipping bowl, beaters and cream in the freezer for 10 minutes only. The result will impress you.

Watermelon Rind Pickles

Some of my fondest childhood memories include eating watermelon rind pickles at my Aunt Gladys' farm. A little nibble now and then brings back wonderful thoughts of fine old lace and excellent turkey dinner.

4-5 pounds watermelon rind, sliced 1" x 1" and pared
4 cups water
½ cup sea salt
2½ cups raw honey
4 cups apple cider vinegar
1 tablespoon plus 12 to garnish whole allspice
1 tablespoon plus 12 to garnish whole cloves
2 sticks cinnamon
1" piece fresh ginger root

Place watermelon rind slices in a large kettle and cover with the water. Parboil for 5 minutes, then cool, drained. Make sure all pink flesh and green skin are removed. Dissolve the salt in the water drained from the rind slices. Pour over the cooled slices, cover loosely and let stand at room temperature for 6 hours or overnight. Drain, rinse and cover with clean water. Simmer until the rind slices are tender, then drain and discard the water. Pour the honey and vinegar over the hot rind slices and stir well. Into a spice bag add the tablespoon of allspice, the tablespoon of cloves, and the cinnamon and ginger. Crush the spice bag with a blunt instrument, then add it to the pot. Simmer for ½ hour, then stir and continue simmering until the rind slices are clear. (Be sure to add extra water as needed to keep the slices covered.) Pack in sterile pint jars as usual, and include 2 whole allspice and two whole cloves to each jar.

Makes 6 pints.

Celestial Conserve

Making conserve is so fast, so easy and so delectable, it has the mess and hassle of jam and jelly beat hands down.

4 oranges, peeled and halved
1 pink grapefruit, peeled and quartered
3 lemons, quartered
8 bananas, peeled and mashed
2½ cups raw honey
1 cup unsweetened coconut, shredded
¾ cup almonds, sliced

Wash, peel and thinly slice the oranges and grapefruit. Wash and thinly slice the lemon. Combine the mashed bananas and the honey in a large saucepan and heat to the boil, stirring constantly. Add the citrus fruits to the banana mixture and simmer 20 minutes, stirring frequently. Add in the coconut and almonds and cook another 3 minutes. Seal in sterile jars as usual.

Makes 6 pints.

Handy Hint: To clean parsley, immerse top down in a large bowl of water to which 1 teaspoon salt has been added. Let stand 15 minutes. Sand and possibly other residents will leave the parsley. Wrap parsley in a paper towel and put in a closed plastic bag. Store in refrigerator. Will keep up to 6 weeks.

Saucy Nectarine Chutney

Some chutney is meant to fight fire with fire. This fruity and spicy chutney will do just that, and be a perfect condiment to your meal.

1½ cups raw honey
½ cup apple cider vinegar
1 teaspoon sea salt
¼ teaspoon cayenne pepper
¼ teaspoon allspice
3 drops Tabasco sauce
4 ripe nectarines, pitted and chopped
2 lemons, seeded and minced
2 medium onions, sliced
½ cup red bell peppers, chopped
¼ cup fresh ginger, grated
   or
⅛ cup crystalized ginger, chopped
¾ cup golden raisins

In a saucepan boil together the raw honey, vinegar and sea salt. Add in the cayenne pepper, allspice and Tabasco sauce. Boil 3 minutes, then add in the nectarines, lemons, onions, red bell pepper and grated ginger. Simmer 10 minutes, stirring frequently. Add in the golden raisins and continue to cook for 25 minutes. Stir occasionally. Seal in sterile jars. Chill and store chilled until served.

Makes 3 pints.

Handy Hint: Don't snap fresh asparagus. You will normally waste about 1" of vegetable. Instead, peel the lower part then gently cut any woody part with a small knife. You can easily tell the tender area from the tough.

Minty Marinated Carrots

An excellent garnish to a main dish or salad, or a perfect vegetable for an hors d'oeuvre tray.

1 fresh mint leaf, washed
¼ cup white vinegar
¼ cup apple cider
2 tablespoons butter
4 large carrots, sliver-cut in 3" strips, peeled

Combine the mint leaf, vinegar, cider and butter in a sauce pan and bring to a boil. Add in the carrots and simmer for 10 minutes, covered, until tender but firm. Remove the mint leaf and discard. Chill the carrots and juice overnight. Serve as a garnish or hors d'oeuvre.

Makes about 3 cups.

Herb Salt

For some people, giving up salt means not eating any more. Quite the contrary when low sodium seasonings taste this great. Sprinkle this mixture on everything from fresh salad greens to scrambled eggs. Before you know it, foods will have their delicious flavors back. And you will have kicked the heavy salt habit enjoyably.

4 tablespoons kelp powder
1 tablespoon basil
2 teaspoons summer savory
2 teaspoons celery seed
2 teaspoons sage
1 teaspoon thyme
   (lemon or pineapple thyme will do)
1 teaspoon marjoram

Combine these ingredients with a mortar and pestle until pulverized. A wooden spoon and a rough finish on a bowl will suffice. A blender will also work. Store in an airtight container with a sprinkle top.

Makes about ½ cup.

You'll Never Eat Store-Bought Again Zucchini Relish

Before I tried zucchini relish, I thought it was just another of those things you made out of zucchini in the last panic-stricken days of October garden harvest. Wrong again, gourmet breath. This food far out-performs sweet cucumber relish. It's well worth the effort.

5 cups zucchini, shredded and packed
2 medium onions, minced
3 tablespoons sea salt
water to cover
½ cup red bell pepper
1¼ cups white vinegar
½ cup raw honey
½ teaspoon celery seed
1 teaspoon turmeric

Shred the zucchini and chop the onions. (If you have a food processor, this is a perfect time to use it.) Combine them with the salt and mix well. Cover with water, then cover and chill overnight. Next day, rinse the salt out of the vegetables with the remaining ingredients and bring to a slow boil. Cook, uncovered, for 1 hour, stirring regularly. When the volume of the relish is reduced to about 1 quart or so, seal in sterile jars.

Makes 4 half pints of excellent relish.

Fresh Cucumber Flourish

This fresh garnish is so delicious, it goes many places. It is perfect as a side garnish with pâté, as an interesting salad pickle, and served atop a cracker with a cream cheese and caviar spread. So many ways, it is the perfect pickle.

3 medium cucumbers
2 tablespoons soy sauce
2 teaspoons raw honey
½ cup red wine vinegar
2 green onion tops, minced
½ cup parsley, minced
3 tablespoons sesame seeds, ground or chopped
1 tablespoon soy oil

Peel the cucumbers and slice in very thin rounds. Place in deep crock, and pour the soy sauce, honey and vinegar over all. Fold in, then sprinkle on green onion, parsley, sesame seed and soy oil. Toss lightly to blend the flavors. Chill for 1 hour, then serve. Top with fresh ground black pepper when serving.

Makes 12 garnishes.

Serving suggestion: This also makes a very tangy salad. Serve on lettuce or spinach leaves.

Serves 4-6.

Handy Hint: Slices of cucumber will refresh tired eyes.

Old Fashioned Brandied Pineapple

Tutti-Frutti is another name for this method of preserving fresh fruits. It is very sweet, and is excellent served on ice cream, light foams and puddings, crepes and breakfast waffles.

5 cups fresh pineapple chunked
2 cups raw honey
1 cup Brandy
1 cup large raisins
24 sweet cherries, pitted and stemmed
12 strawberries, firm and capped

In a two-gallon crock with a loose-fitting lid, mix together the pineapple, raw honey and Brandy until the honey is dissolved. Add in the raisins, cherries and strawberries and gently fold in. Set the crock on the kitchen counter and stir gently every day for two weeks. Seal in sterile pint jars as usual, or store in the refrigerator until serving time.

Variation: For added visual effect and a tropical twist, add in ½ cup shredded, unsweetened coconut at canning time.

Makes 6 pints.

Mango Easy Chutney

Chutney is an accompaniment to spicy meals which accents the food and helps cool the fire of the main dish. At its best, chutney is fresh, tangy and easy to make. Serve chutney on a small Lazy Susan with the other condiments to your meal.

4 medium mangoes, ripe
juice of 1 lemon
1 tablespoon grated lemon rind
3 tablespoons raw honey
½ teaspoon grated ginger root

Peel and chunk the mango flesh from the inner seed. Chop coarsely. Place in a glass bowl, and sprinkle with the lemon juice, lemon rind, raw honey and grated fresh ginger. Toss, cover and chill until serving.

Note: You may want to reduce this recipe for a smaller meal, or simply seal in sterile pint jars and preserve the remainder for winter!

Makes 3½ cups.

Handy Hint: When a vegetable is accidentally overcooked, make a puree of it, place in a baking dish, top with cheese and bake 15 minutes. Serve.

SOUPS, SAUCES

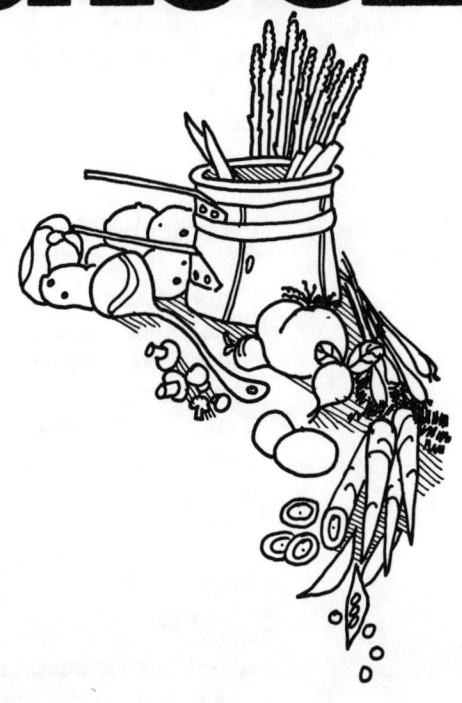

Cream of Leek Soup

2 cups leeks, slivered (white part only)
1 cup carrot, slivered
1 cup onion, minced
¼ cup celery, minced
¼ cup butter
1 tablespoon olive oil
4 potatoes, scrubbed and thinly sliced
6 cups stock
1 cup heavy cream
1 teaspoon oyster sauce
pepper to taste
1 teaspoon miso
1 tablespoon chives, minced

Saute the leeks, carrot, onion and celery together in heated butter and olive oil. Toss lightly to coat all ingredients. When leeks are limp and onion is translucent, add in potatoes and toss to cover them with oil also. Add in stock and heat to a boil. Reduce heat and simmer 45 minutes. Whisk in the cream, oyster sauce, pepper and miso and heat but do not boil. Serve with chive garnish.

Serves 6.

Handy Hint: When there is no time to cool and skim stock before using it, drop a few ice cubes into the stock. Within 10 minutes the fat will stick to the cubes and it can be easily removed.

Whole Protein Yellow Split Pea Soup

1 cup yellow peas
½ cup garbanzo beans
⅛ cup millet
⅛ cup peanuts, raw
8 cups stock
1 cup onion, minced
2 cloves garlic, bruised
3 tablespoons olive oil
1 tablespoon miso
1 medium carrot, chopped

Combine the peas, beans, millet and peanuts with the stock and bring to a boil. Cover and simmer 1 hour. Saute the onion and garlic in the heated olive oil. When tender, add in the miso and carrot pieces. Stir-fry 1 minute, then add to soup mixture. Mix in well, then simmer another hour. Let stand, covered for 30 minutes, then puree in blender or food processor. Reheat if necessary and serve.

Makes 12 servings.

Succotash Corn Chowder

½ cup zucchini, chopped
¼ cup onion, chopped
2 tablespoons butter
1 cup corn
½ cup apples, cored and sliced
½ teaspoon curry powder
¼ teaspoon nutmeg
1 tablespoon Sherry
2 cups lima beans, cooked
6 cups stock
pepper to taste

Saute the zucchini and onion in butter until tender. Add in the remaining ingredients and bring to a boil. Simmer 2 hours.

Serves 10.

Cream of Cauliflower Soup

1 tablespoon shallots, minced
1 tablespoon butter
1 teaspoon safflower oil
2 pounds cauliflower, cleaned and pared, then thinly sliced
6 cups stock
2/3 cup long grain brown rice
1 cup milk
1½ cups half and half
1 cup undyed cheddar cheese, shredded
1/8 teaspoon nutmeg
1/8 teaspoon curry
3 drops Tabasco
pepper to taste

Saute shallots in butter and oil until translucent. Add in sliced cauliflower and toss to coat. Add in stock and rice. Cover, bring to a boil and simmer 45 minutes. Add in milk, half and half and cheese and stir in well. Add in all seasonings and simmer 10 minutes, stirring frequently. Let stand, covered 15 minutes.

Variation: If you prefer, this soup may be pureed. It is excellent either way.

Serves 6-8.

Old Fashioned Tomato-Rice Soup

8½ cups stock
2 tablespoons butter
1 teaspoon safflower oil
1 large onion, chopped
¼ cup celery, chopped
½ cup zucchini, chopped
2 tablespoons green pepper, minced
1 small garlic clove, bruised
¼ cup carrot, chopped
1 tablespoon parsley, chopped
9 large tomatoes (just under 4 pounds), peeled, seeded, chopped
1/3 cup long grain brown rice
½ teaspoon thyme
pinch oregano
1 teaspoon herb salt
pepper

Make stock if necessary. (see index) Heat butter and oil until foamy. When foam ceases, saute onion, celery, zucchini, green pepper, garlic, carrot and parsley until onion is tender. Add in tomatoes and 1 cup of stock and simmer 15 minutes. Add in 3 more cups broth and simmer, covered for 30-35 minutes. Remove from the heat and puree the soup mixture. Return to the heat and add the remaining stock and the rice and seasonings. Return to the boil, and simmer 10 minutes. Turn off the heat but leave the soup to steep, covered for 1 hour. Check that the rice is tender. Serve after reheating slightly.

Note: This soup may be served chilled as a refreshing summer soup. Garnish with shredded cucumber for the perfect touch.

Serves 10.

Handy Hint: Keep your vegetables fresher longer. Add a sponge to the vegetable drawer of the refrigerator.

Viennese Barley Soup

⅓ cup pearl barley
¾ cup onion, minced
¼ cup celery, minced
1 small garlic clove, pressed
2 tablespoons butter
1 teaspoon safflower oil
1 tablespoon whole wheat pastry flour
1 teaspoon soy sauce
4½ cups stock
¼ cup heavy cream
2 tablespoons parsley, minced
4 lemon slices, very thin

Saute the barley, onion, celery and garlic in the heated butter and oil until the onion is tender and the barley is translucent. Avoid browning. Whisk in the flour then add in the soy sauce and stock. Stir constantly to ensure smoothness, about 1 minute. Heat to boiling, then simmer, covered for about an hour. Have cream at room temperature, and add it in slowly. Heat back to the boiling point, but do not boil. Serve immediately with a lemon wedge and parsley garnish. Pepper to taste.

Serves 4.

Handy Hint: When too much water has been added to soup, making it too thin, simply add in some leftover mashed potatoes to thicken it up again.

Green Goddess Soup

1 tablespoon safflower oil
1 clove garlic, minced or pressed
½ cup onion, chopped
2 ripe avocados, large
¼ cup lemon juice
2½ cups vegetable broth or chicken broth
¼ teaspoon Tabasco sauce
2 tablespoons parsley, minced
1½ cups milk
½ cup plain yogurt
½ teaspoon soy sauce

Saute garlic and onion in butter until tender. Cool slightly. Peel, pit and chop avocados and place in blender together with the onion mixture and lemon juice. Whip until very smooth, then trickle in the broth and continue whipping until all is included. Pour into a glass bowl and fold in the Tabasco, parsley, milk, plain yogurt and soy sauce. Stir until well-mixed. Cover and chill for at least 1 hour, then serve.

Serves 6.

Egg Flower Soup

A soup of distinction for centuries.

4 cups chicken broth
½ cup water chestnuts, finely sliced
3 mushrooms, finely sliced
2 eggs, lightly beaten
1 green onion, finely sliced

Combine the broth and water chestnuts and boil about 5 minutes. Add in the sliced mushrooms. Stir soup with a chopstick, and slowly drizzle the scrambled eggs into the broth. Stir gently so egg forms "flowers." Quickly add in green onion, stir once and serve.

Serves 4.

Fumet (Classic fish or game broth)

This full-bodied stock is perfect for addition to recipes, and may also be served as a clear soup for a formal meal. Pay careful attention to the straining.

1 pound fish bones and trimmings
1 carrot, chopped
1 small onion, chopped
¼ cup parsley, chopped
¼ cup butter
1½ cups water
1 cup white wine
3 peppercorns, crushed
½ teaspoon soy sauce

Place all ingredients in a covered saucepan and bring to a boil. Reduce the heat and simmer for 30 minutes. Rinse a cheesecloth in cold water, and line a strainer with it. Place over another bowl, and strain the soup. Chill the strained liquid; discard the solid waste.

Makes 2½ cups fumet.

Russian Sauerkraut Soup

2½ cups sauerkraut
4 cups stock or water
2 carrots, sliver-sliced
1 pound smoked meat or smoked tofu
2 tablespoons whole wheat pastry flour
1 teaspoon honey
1 teaspoon Dijon mustard
2 tablespoons ketchup or tomato sauce
pepper to taste

Combine the sauerkraut, stock and carrots in a large, covered pot and bring to a boil. Reduce the heat and simmer 1 hour. Add in the smoked meat and stir once. Combine the last four ingredients in a small bowl and stir until smooth. Add into the soup, stirring thoroughly. Pepper to taste. Cover and simmer 10 minutes, then serve.

Serves 6-8.

Continental Shelf Bisque

¼ pound scallops
¼ pound shrimp
¼ pound small lobster tails
3 tablespoons celery, minced
2 tablespoons shallots, minced
3 tablespoons butter
1½ teaspoons safflower oil
2 tablespoons whole wheat pastry flour
½ teaspoon soy sauce
⅛ teaspoon white pepper
1½ cups chicken broth or fumet (see index)
1½ cups light cream
½ teaspoon oyster sauce (see index)
½ cup parsley, minced

Clean and pat dry the shellfish. Mince. Saute the celery and shallots in the heated butter and safflower oil until tender. Add in the fish and saute 3 minutes more, stirring occasionally. Sprinkle in the flour and stir well. Add soy sauce and pepper, then slowly add in the broth and light cream. Stir in the oyster sauce, and allow the soup to simmer until thickened, about 5 minutes. Remove from the heat and puree in a blender in small batches. Serve immediately, garnished with parsley.

Variation: This bisque may also be served chilled. Simply chill after pureeing, and serve in chilled bowls, garnished as above.

Serves 4.

Fresh Pumpkin Soup

3 cups steamed pumpkin flesh, mashed
¾ cup apple juice
¼ cup white wine
2 cups vegetable stock
1 cup heavy cream
2 tablespoons lemon juice
1 teaspoon blackstrap molasses
dash curry powder
dash nutmeg
½ cup carrot, shredded
½ teaspoon herbed vinegar

Combine the pumpkin flesh, apple juice, wine and stock and bring to a boil in an uncovered pot. Reduce heat and simmer 20 minutes. Cool 15 minutes, then process in blender or food processor until smooth. Return the mixture to the cooking pot. Add in the heavy cream, lemon juice, molasses and seasonings. Carefully heat just to steaming, stirring occasionally. Cover and set aside 3 minutes. Meanwhile, combine the shredded carrot with the vinegar and stir well. Ladle the soup into bowls and garnish with the carrot mixture.

Serves 4-6.

Terry's Oyster Stew

1 pint small oysters, cleaned
3 tablespoons celery, minced
2 tablespoons shallots, minced
¼ cup butter
2 teaspoons safflower oil
½ teaspoon soy sauce
dash pepper, fresh ground
3 cups whole milk
1 tablespoon white wine
¼ cup parsley, minced
4 lemon slices, very thin

Pat dry the oysters. If they are large, cut up slightly. Saute the celery and shallots in heated butter and oil until tender. Add in the oysters and continue to saute until the oysters curl at the sides. Add in seasonings, milk and wine and heat to simmering. Simmer, covered for 1 minute. Ladle into bowls, garnish with parsley and float lemon slice on top of soup at side of parsley.

Serves 4.

Handy Hint: To add a touch of class to simmering foods, add a splash of wine during the final 30 minutes of cooking. Do not cover: allow the alcohol fumes to escape.

Springtime Radish Soup

The radish is seen as a salad vegetable, eaten raw. This fresh radish soup will take you to a new dimension of pleasure with the earliest of garden crops.

3 cups stock or water
   (if water, add 1 teaspoon mild miso)
2 slices ginger root, 1" long
1 garlic clove, bruised
2 cups red radish, shredded
1 tablespoon lemon juice
3 tablespoons plain yogurt
1 tablespoon minced chives
1 teaspoon lemon zest

Bring the stock to a boil, add in the ginger and garlic and simmer for 30 minutes. Remove the ginger and garlic. Add in the shredded radish and lemon juice and stir evenly for one minute. Remove from the heat and whisk in the yogurt. Ladle into serving bowls and garnish with chives and lemon zest.

Note: The light pink color of this soup can be a special feature for a colorful meal. Consider a fresh fruit juice like strawberry-apple to accompany it.

Serves 4.

Fast Manhattan Chowder

¼ pound scallops
¼ pound clams, chopped or ground
½ cup onion, chopped
½ cup green pepper, minced
1 clove garlic, pressed
1 cup celery, chopped
¼ cup safflower oil
1 cup water
1 cup potatoes, diced
¼ teaspoon thyme
½ teaspoon sea salt
⅛ teaspoon pepper
2½ cups cocktail vegetable juice
½ cup tofu, minced (optional)

Clean and pat dry the scallops and clams. Saute the onion, green pepper, garlic, and celery in hot safflower oil until tender. Add in the shellfish and saute 2 more minutes. Add in the water, potatoes and seasonings and bring to a boil. Cook 15 minutes, then add in the vegetable juice and tofu and simmer 5 minutes.

Serves 4-5.

Handy Hint: After obtaining juice from a lemon half, keep it at the sink for a fast de-greasing job on whatever comes along. Use especially in a bowl just before whipping egg whites or whipping cream. Be sure to rinse and dry first.

Parisienne Onion Soup

3 cups onion, thin-sliced
¼ cup butter
2 teaspoons safflower oil
6 cups vegetable stock
1 tablespoon white wine
pepper to taste
½ teaspoon soy sauce
6 French bread rounds, toasted
3 cups, Emmentaler or other
  Swiss cheese, shredded

Saute onions in heated butter and oil until translucent. Add in stock and wine and simmer 20 minutes. Stir in pepper and soy sauce. Ladle into onion soup crocks or oven-proof soup bowls. Top with toasted bread and cheese. Bake in oven at 400 for 10 minutes or until cheese is golden and bubbly. Serve immediately.

Serves 6.

Vegetable Stock

This broth or stock may be used anywhere a "stock or broth" is called for in cooking. You may use "potato water" instead of water in this recipe, as well as vegetable peelings, onion tops, garlic skin and any other vegetable parts discarded for their lack of total attractiveness.

8 cups water
½ cup carrot, chopped
½ cup celery, chopped
½ cup onion, chopped
1 garlic clove, bruised
1 small potato, minced (leave out for clear broth)
6 peppercorns

Bring all ingredients to a boil in a covered pot, then simmer 30 minutes. Strain and chill. Store covered in the refrigerator.
Variation: For a chicken broth or heartier, meaty flavor, add chicken bones or beef bones to the broth. For the beef bones, mince the marrow into the liquid for full flavor advantage. About 1 pound bones will do.

Makes 2 quarts.

Standard Quick Stock

One of the easiest ways to make a fast soup stock is with the use of miso (mee-sow), a fermented grain paste full of protein and flavor. It is high in salt content, so never use more than 1 tablespoon for every four cups liquid in stock. If your soup still lacks flavor at that point, re-examine the flavor and quality of your ingredients, but do not increase the miso to compensate. Miso is available at natural food stores and Oriental grocery stores. Dashi, a dried broth base, is also useful. Most dashi envelopes are for 4 cups liquid also, but some are for individual servings. Check the directions on the package before proceeding.

4 cups water
2 teaspoons miso
1 sprig celery leaves
1 garlic clove, bruised
3 peppercorns

Bring the ingredients to a boil and simmer 5 minutes. Allow to cool, then strain. Store in a covered glass jar in the refrigerator until needed. May be used anytime in this book where "stock" is called for.

Makes 4 cups.

Dipping Sauce for Sashimi
(Japanese Raw Fish)

Sashimi, thin sliced raw fish, is served on a bed of lettuce with a dipping sauce to the side. Most commonly used fish include yellow-fin tuna (pink translucent), salmon and red snapper.

2 teaspoons Wasabi powder
   (green mustard powder)
1 tablespoon water
2 tablespoons soy sauce
1 tablespoon vinegar
   (rice wine vinegar if possible)
4 drops honey

Combine wasabi powder and water and let stand 5 minutes. Whisk in the soy sauce, vinegar and honey and serve.

Note: Wasabi is very powerful mustard, so when using it for other purposes such as egg roll dipping or barbecue pork dipping, be as careful as you are with the hot yellow Chinese mustard.

Makes ¼ cup.

Tempura Dipping Sauce

1 cup soy sauce
¼ cup Chinese Black Vinegar
   or
Worcestershire sauce
2 tablespoons garlic, minced
2 tablespoons ginger root, shredded
½ cup water
1 tablespoon sesame oil

Whisk all ingredients together and let stand, covered, 4 hours. Strain and store in the cupboard, covered. This sauce is perfect for dipping egg roll, dim sum and hom bow also.

Variation: For a hot and spicy version, add in 2 tablespoons Hot Pepper Oil (see index).

Makes 2 cups sauce.

Chinese Oyster Sauce

6 fresh oysters, medium
2 cups soy sauce
1 teaspoon sea salt

Chop the oysters and pat them dry. Combine the oysters, soy sauce and salt in a small covered saucepan and boil lightly for 1 hour. Cool and strain twice. Store the liquid in a covered jar in the cupboard. This sauce is used to give a general enhancing effect to cooking. It works particularly well in meat dishes and soups. It does not give an "oyster" taste.

Makes about 2 cups.

Handy Hint: For hands that pick up onion, fish, and garlic smell while cooking, rub with lemon juice, toothpaste, baking soda or prepared mustard for instant relief.

Hot Pepper Oil

5 dried red chilis, about 4" long
½ cup safflower oil

Heat oil in a small frying pan. Cut chilis into 4 lengthwise pieces and fry in the oil until the chilis turn very dark. Discard the chilis and strain the oil. Store with a tight stopper in the cupboard. This hot pepper oil may be used like Tabasco sauce, and is best added to other oils while sauteing vegetables. In Asian cooking calling for hot pepper oil, this is it.

Makes about ½ cup oil.

Sweet and Sour Won Ton Dipping Sauce

6 tablespoons ketchup
  or
Refreshing Tomato Sauce (see index)
6 tablespoons water
4 tablespoons honey
2 tablespoons rice vinegar
2 teaspoons soy sauce
2 teaspoons cornstarch
1 tablespoon water

In a small saucepan combine the ketchup, water, honey and rice vinegar. Bring to a boil and simmer 1 minute. Add in the soy sauce. Whisk together the cornstarch and water until dissolved. Add to the heated mixture, whisking briskly until thickened. Simmer 1 minute. Serve hot or chilled with fried won ton, onion rings, french fries made with sweet potatoes or chicken with pineapple.

Makes 1½ cups.

Secret Black Bean Sauce

This is a great "secret sauce" to amaze your guests' palates. The secret ingredient, fermented black beans (commonly found in Oriental sections), offers such a satisfying yet curious difference to the sauce that you need only serve and smile. This recipe makes enough to handle about 2 pounds of meat, cooked. Will also serve as a barbecue sauce, applied half-way through the cooking.

3 tablespoons fermented black beans, canned
⅓ green onion, minced
2 tablespoons ginger root, fresh grated
1 tablespoon garlic, minced
⅔ cup stock or water
⅓ cup soy sauce
¼ cup Sherry or Sake
1 tablespoon honey
¼ cup peanut oil

Soak the beans in water to cover for 15 minutes, then drain and mince. Put all ingredients in a small saucepan and stir to mix well. Heat the mixture to a boil, then simmer 15 minutes, stirring frequently until thick.

Makes about 2 cups sauce.

Classic Caper Sauce

1 cup parsley, minced
½ cup pine nuts
½ cup capers, drained
1 slice whole grain bread
2 tablespoons red wine vinegar
1 garlic clove, pressed
½ cup olive oil

Fill a large bowl with water and 1 teaspoon salt. Soak parsley for 5 minutes before mincing to release lodged sand and various high-protein residents. Rinse, pat dry and mince the parsley. Pack the parsley into the cup, then combine it with the pine nuts, capers and torn bread pieces into a blender or food processor. Blend until mixed. Add in vinegar, garlic and olive oil and process until smooth. This sauce may be served room temperature or chilled with seafoods, roast meats, sauteed mushrooms or stuffed tomatoes. It is also interesting served as a dressing on a chilled pasta salad. (see index)

Makes 2 cups.

Red Soy Sauce

3 tablespoons honey
1 tablespoon blackstrap molasses
¼ cup soy sauce
½ stick cinnamon
3 star anise
1 teaspoon sesame oil

Combine all ingredients in a small saucepan and bring to a boil. Simmer 15 minutes. Let stand 5 minutes, covered, then strain and cool. Store covered in the cupboard until served. This sauce is used as a food dip for hom bow, shumai, egg rolls and poultry.

Makes ½ cup.

Refreshing Tomato Sauce

6 tomatoes, large
4 tablespoons apple cider vinegar
3 tablespoons olive oil
1 tablespoon tarragon
¼ teaspoon mint leaves

Clean, peel, seed and chop the tomatoes. Force through a sieve or ricer. Place sieved tomatoes in a glass bowl and whisk briefly while adding in the vinegar. Continue whisking and add the olive oil in a slow and steady stream. Include the tarragon and mint and blend in well. Sauce should have consistancy of thick ketchup. Thin with water if necessary, 1 teaspoon at a time. Chill in a covered bowl until served. Particularly delicious served beside pâté.

Makes 2 cups.

Creamy Horseradish Sauce

1½ cups plain yogurt
2 tablespoons whole wheat bread crumbs
1 tablespoon horseradish,
    prepared or fresh grated
2 teaspoons Dijon-style mustard
pepper to taste

Whip together in a small glass bowl until well blended. Chill, covered, for 1 hour before serving. Excellent served with sausage, roast beef, borscht, as a garnish on stuffed mushrooms.

Makes 2 cups.

Pesto (Green Pasta Sauce)

3 cups basil leaves, fresh and packed
1 cup pine nuts
1 cup parsley, chopped
¾ cup Parmesan cheese, grated
½ cup olive oil
1 clove garlic, pressed
½ cup olive oil, to seal

Wash and pat dry the basil leaves. Remove any stems. In a blender or food processor blend until smooth the basil leaves, pine nuts, parsley, Parmesan cheese, ½ cup olive oil and garlic. Store in a quart jar, trying not to spill down the inside of the jar. Top the pesto with ½ cup olive oil to seal out the air until used.

Makes about 2 cups. This recipe will top ½ pound pasta and serve 4.

Classic Teriyaki Marinade

¼ cup soy sauce
¼ cup orange juice
½ teaspoon ginger root, shredded
1 teaspoon honey
2 garlic cloves, bruised

Combine all ingredients in a blender and liquify completely. Heat to a boil in a small saucepan, then simmer 1 minute. Remove from heat and cool.

Makes about ½ cup. (Will marinate 2-3 pounds meat.)

Walnut Marinade

2 tablespoons white vinegar
1 tablespoon light olive oil
pinch salt
½ cup walnut oil
¼ cup walnut meats, powdered

Whisk vigorously in a glass bowl for 2 minutes. Marinate up to 2 pounds of mushrooms or other soft vegetables such as zucchini, pearl onions or peas for several hours. (May also be used as a salad dressing over light greens. Use sparingly.)

Makes 1 cup marinade.

Mainland Luau Marinade

For a large luau dinner, I marinated various vegetables in one container and sliced chicken breast in another container all day long. When the charcoal was ready I let my guests make their own skewer masterpieces and the meal was ready to go.

½ cup soy sauce
½ cup pineapple juice
1 tablespoon onion, shredded
1 tablespoon ginger root, shredded
2 tablespoons sesame seed
½ cup safflower oil
4 drops Tabasco
⅛ teaspoon pepper
2 teaspoons oyster sauce
1 tablespoon honey
2 tablespoons papaya, mashed

Whiz all ingredients together in the blender for 1 minute. Pour over vegetables and meats of your choice.

Makes 2½ cups, or enough for about 6 pounds of food. (Reserve the leftovers for a dipping sauce at the table.)

Sublime Marinade

¼ cup Hoisin sauce
3 tablespoons rice wine (Sake or Mirin)
2 tablespoons green onion
2 tablespoons soy sauce
2 garlic cloves, pressed
1 teaspoon honey
1 teaspoon ginger root, grated

Whisk all ingredients together in a small bowl. Let stand overnight in refrigerator. This strong marinade is perfect for overnight refrigerated marinating. It works well on beef, pork and fowl. It may be used straight or strained, depending upon your interest in extraneous ingredients in the ultimate recipe.

Makes about ½ cup.

SALADS, DRESSINGS

Tangy Tomato Aspic

2 cups tomatoes, peeled, seeded and minced
1 envelope unflavored gelatin
1 tablespoon lemon juice
1 tablespoon lime juice
2 tablespoons parsley, minced
2 tablespoons fresh basil, minced
or
2 teaspoons dried basil
1 tablespoon celery leaves, minced
1 tablespoon red onion, minced
2 tablepoons cucumber, minced
8 Romaine leaves, large
1 cup zucchini, shredded

Combine the tomatoes and their juice together with the gelatin in a small saucepan. Allow the gelatin to soften a few minutes, then simmer 4 minutes. Set aside and cool. Once room temperature, add in the lemon and lime juices, parsley, basil, celery leave, onion and cucumber. Mix well, then pour into a 3 cup-mold and chill 4 hours. When set, turn onto a platter covered with the Romaine. Garnish with the shredded zucchini and serve.

Serves 4-6.

The Perfect Caesar Salad

2 cloves garlic, bruised
½ cup light olive oil
2 Romaine, solid heads, washed and crisped
2 tablespoons lemon juice
½ cup Parmesan cheese, freshly grated
3 anchovy fillets, minced
1 tablespoon vinegar
1 raw egg (may use 1-minute coddled egg)
1 cup croutons (see below to make your own)

Marinate oil with garlic cloves for about 1½ hours before proceeding. Meanwhile clean, pat dry and wrap Romaine in toweling and crisp in the refrigerator 1 hour. Remove and tear into bowl. Remove garlic from oil and mix with lemon juice. Let stand aside. Sprinkle cheese and anchovies over lettuce, whip vinegar with oil and pour over lettuce. Toss salad lightly until all is coated well. Make a well in the middle of the salad. Lightly whisk the egg and pour into the well. Gently toss the salad until the leaves glisten. Top with croutons and serve immediately. (It is most appealing to do the final assembly in front of your dinner guests. It is smart, however, not to point out the addition of anchovies since your guests will enjoy the dish more if not trying to single out a foreign-sounding ingredient!)

Serves 6.

Croutons

1 cup cubed French bread, dried out
1½ tablespoons butter
1 tablespoon olive oil
1 clove garlic, bruised

Saute bruised garlic in butter and oil until browned. Remove, and saute bread cubes until toasty. Cool slightly and add to salad. (You may want to make croutons for other uses, in which case the addition of 1 teaspoon of parsley or mixed herbs is appropriate when the bread goes in.)

Velvety Avocado Mousse

3 cups miso stock (see Index)
2 envelopes unflavored gelatin
2 avocados, pared and pitted
¼ cup lime juice
1 teaspoon parsley, minced
1 teaspoon chives, minced
10-12 cucumber slices
1 cup alfalfa sprouts, for garnish
⅓ cup plain yogurt
1 tablespoon milk
¼ cup walnuts, minced

Combine the stock and gelatin and let dissolve 5 minutes. Heat to the boil, simmer 3 minutes and cool to room temperature. Add half the stock to a blender, together with the avocados, lime juice, parsley and chives. Whip until pureed. Return the avocado mixture to the remaining stock and chill, covered until ¾ set. Remove from the refrigerator and whip to mix completely. Arrange cucumber slices in a 6 cup mold, then pour avocado mixture in. Cover and chill 1 hour, or until set. Unmold onto a platter and garnish at the base with alfalfa sprouts. Make a dressing of the yogurt, milk and walnuts and pour over all. Serve immediately.

Serves 6.

Molded Gazpacho

1 cup miso stock
3 envelopes unflavored gelatin
2 cups cocktail vegetable juice
  (may use spicy variety)
¼ cup lime juice
2 tablespoons lemon juice
1 red bell pepper, chopped
½ green pepper, minced
1 tomato, peeled, seeded and chopped
½ cup avocado, chopped
2 cups cucumber, peeled and seeded (if large)
3 green onions, minced
½ cup red onion, minced
1 tablespoon chives, minced
2 tablespoons parsley, minced
1 teaspoon soy sauce
4 drops Tabasco sauce
sprigs of parsley for garnish
celery sticks for garnish

Combine the miso stock, gelatin and vegetable juice and let stand 5 minutes. Heat to a boil, then remove from heat and let come to room temperature. Add in lemon and lime juices and stir well. Chill, covered, until half-set. Remove and add all the chopped vegetables and herbs, together with the soy sauce and Tabasco. Stir well, and pour into a 6-8 cup mold. Chill 6 hours or overnight, until firm. Unmold and garnish with parsley and celery.

Note: This may also be served in a wine glass with a celery and parsley garnish and an iced tea spoon as a refreshing patio first course. Ole!

Serves 8.

Handy Hint: Mashed avocado or peach will serve well as a moisturizing masque.

Fourth of July Marinated Salad

1 cup kidney beans, cooked
½ cup garbanzo beans, cooked
1 cup green beans, cooked
¾ cup long grain brown rice, cooked
¼ cup celery, minced
¼ cup green pepper, sliced
½ cup tomato wedges
¼ cup green olives, pitted
1 medium red onion, ring sliced
1 clove garlic
1 teaspoon salt
¼ cup olive oil
1½ tablespoons red wine vinegar
2 teaspoons honey
2 teaspoons basil, fresh minced

Assemble the salad ingredients in a large glass bowl. Bruise, then mince the garlic. Pour the salt over it and combine the two into a paste. Whisk together the oil, vinegar, honey and basil in a small bowl. Add in the garlic and whip vigorously 1 minute. Pour over the salad and toss well, coating all ingredients. Serve immediately.

Makes 4-5 generous main course servings.

Italian Seafood Salad

¼ cup pitted black olives, sliced coarsley
1 pound crab, cracked and patted dry
½ cup pimento-stuffed green olives
¼ cup parsley, minced
1 tablespoon lemon juice
½ cup mayonnaise
½ cup plain yogurt
pepper to taste
½ cup tiny, cute pasta
1 medium avocado, sliced

Combine both olives, crab, parsley and lemon juice gently and chill, covered for 1½ hours. Whisk together the mayonnaise, yogurt and pepper and chill covered for 1½ hours. In the meantime, bring 2 cups water to the boil and cook the pasta until 'al dente.'* Drain, rinse in cool water and allow to cool covered in the refrigerator. Combine the chilled crab mixture, chilled dressing and chilled pasta and mix completely. Garnish with avocado slices and serve immediately. This salad is also perfect on a buffet.

*literally, "to the teeth" - when it has firm texture yet is cooked.

Serves 6 as a main course.

Spinach-Nasturtium Salad

Flowers make the most glorious additions to salads. Those most often used in salads include roses, violets, geraniums, nasturtiums, marigolds and chrysanthemums. Try some in your next salad.

1 pound spinach
⅛ cup nasturtium flowers, shredded
6 mushrooms, medium
1 egg, hard-cooked and grated
1 teaspoon chives, minced
1 tablespoon red wine vinegar
1 tablespoon lemon juice
¼ cup light olive oil
1 teaspoon honey
pepper to taste

Wash and pat dry the spinach leaves. Tear into salad bowl, then top with nasturtiums. Slice the mushrooms, and add together with the grated egg and chives. Whisk the remaining ingredients together in a small bowl, then dress the salad just before serving.

Makes 6 servings.

Fresh Spring Pea Mousse

1 cup boiling water
2 envelopes unflavored gelatin
2 cups fresh peas, steamed and cooled
2 tablespoons parsley, minced
½ teaspoon soy sauce
¼ teaspoon paprika
dash pepper
½ cup feta, crumbled
1 cup plain yogurt

Combine the water and gelatin in a blender and whip 30 seconds. Add in the peas and seasonings and blend again until the peas are pureed, about 1 minute. Finally, add in the feta and yogurt while the blender is running and blend only until completely combined. Pour mixture into a 3-cup, buttered mold and chill about 3 hours.

Serves 4.

Seviche Mazatlan

2 pounds sole fillets
1 cup lemon juice
¾ cup lime juice
2 large red onions, chopped
4 tomatoes, peeled and wedged
2 tablespoons parsley, minced
2 tablespoons vinegar
1 teaspoon oregano
½ teaspoon lemon zest
¾ cup stuffed green olives, chopped
1 cup cocktail vegetable juice
6 drops Tabasco sauce
1 teaspoon pepper
½ teaspoon soy sauce
½ cup olive oil

Wash fish and cut into ½" cubes. Pat dry, then combine with lemon and lime juices in a glass bowl. Cover and chill overnight. In a large salad bowl, combine the salad ingredients. Whisk the vegetable juice, Tabasco, pepper, soy sauce and oil together. Drain the fish, then add to the salad ingredients. Pour the dressing overall and mix well. Cover and chill 1 hour, then serve.

Makes 12 servings.

Osaka Salad

8 Shiitake mushrooms
1 cup water, hot
¼ cup water
1 tablespoon soy oil
1 teaspoon honey
¼ cup miso stock, double strength
½ cup soy oil
½ cup rice vinegar
¼ cup honey
1 teaspoon sesame oil
2 eggs
1 tablespoon soy oil
8 ounces soba noodles, dry
10 inch cucumber, julienne-cut
2 tablespoons green onion, minced

Soak the mushrooms in 1 cup water, then julienne slice. Discard any extra moisture. Combine ¼ cup water, 1 tablespoon oil and 1 teaspoon honey and bring to a boil, simmering 3 minutes. Add in the mushrooms, cover and cool 45 minutes. Combine ¼ cup miso stock, ½ cup soy oil, ½ cup rice vinegar, ¼ cup honey and 1 teaspoon sesame oil and boil. Reduce heat and simmer 5 minutes. Cover and chill 20 minutes. Whip eggs well, then pour into small pan heated with 1 tablespoon soy oil and let cook without stirring firm. Remove with a spatula and cool, then cut into julienne strips. Heat 2 quarts water to a boil and cook soba until al dente, then drain, rinse with cold water and refrigerate 2½ hours, covered. Toss noodles with chilled cup of sauce and divide among serving dishes. Decorate noodles with mushrooms, egg strips, cucumber slices and minced onion. Serve immediately.

Makes 8 salads.

Beijing Chicken Salad

4 medium chicken breasts, skinned
2 tablespoons smooth peanut butter
2 tablespoons orange juice
2 tablespoons soy sauce
1½ tablespoons white vinegar
1 tablespoon sesame oil
1 tablespoon dry white wine
2 teaspoons honey
¼ cup green onion, minced
2 teaspoons red ginger, or shredded ginger root
4 cups crispy chow mein noodles
2 cups iceberg lettuce, shredded and patted dry
2 teaspoons black sesame seeds

Heat 4 cups water to a boil and immerse the chicken breasts. Poach 12 minutes, until tender, then remove and cool. (Save water for stock in another recipe.) In a bowl whisk together the peanut butter, juice and other liquid ingredients. When well mixed add in the onion and ginger and stir gently to coat. Dice the chicken meat and combine with the crispy noodles and lettuce in a large bowl. Toss gently then sprinkle with sesame seeds and dressing. Toss to wet all ingredients and serve immediately.

Serves 4 main course salads or up to 8 smaller salads.

Antipasto Vege'

1½ cups frozen corn kernels
1 red pepper, sliced
1 cup mushrooms, sliced
½ cup green onion, julienne strips
1 jar marinated artichoke hearts, reserve juice
3 tablespoons vinegar
1 garlic clove, bruised
½ teaspoon oregano
½ teaspoon soy sauce
10 Romaine leaves, patted dry
¼ cup Romano cheese, grated

Combine corn, peppers, mushrooms and green onion together. Pour artichoke juice into small bowl. Add artichokes, cut in half, into corn mixture. To juice add vinegar, garlic, oregano, soy sauce. Puree in blender and pour over corn mixture. Toss well, cover and chill 3 hours. Serve on Romaine leaves and garnish with cheese.

Serves 5.

Spinach Sauerkraut Salad

1 large onion, minced
2 tablespoons butter
1 teaspoon safflower oil
1 teaspoon soy sauce
½ teaspoon caraway seed, crushed
2 bunches spinach, cleaned and patted dry
¾ cup sauerkraut, drained
½ cup mushrooms, chopped
½ cup raw cashews

Saute the onion in hot butter and oil until tender. Garnish with caraway and soy sauce and stir, then remove from the heat and chill 15 minutes. In salad bowl combine spinach, kraut, mushrooms and cashews and toss lightly. Add in chilled onions with all juices and toss well. Serve immediately.

Serves 4.

Hot Taco Salad Acapulco

2 cups red snapper, cooked
1 small onion, chopped
1 tablespoon butter
1 teaspoon safflower oil
8 ounces tomato sauce
½ cup stuffed green olives, chopped
¼ teaspoon Tabasco sauce
   (adjust to personal taste)
½ teaspoon sea salt
3 tablespoons safflower oil
8 corn tortillas
2 cups guacamole
½ cup sour cream
4 cups iceberg lettuce, shredded

Separate fish with fork so it looks flaked. Saute onion in heated butter and oil until onion is translucent, then add in tomato sauce, olives, Tabasco and sea salt. Heat to a boil and simmer 15 minutes. Add in fish, cover and simmer 2 minutes. Fry tortillas lightly in 3 tablespoons oil, and spread on a platter. Spread with fish sauce, then top with guacamole and sour cream. Garnish with lettuce and serve.

Makes 8, but serves 4 for dinner course.

(Guacamole: Combine 2 large avocados, 1 teaspoon minced onion, 1 tablespoon lemon juice, dash of garlic powder, pepper to taste and 1 dash hot sauce in blender and puree. Chill. Makes 2 cups.)

Brown Rice Tabouli

1 cup short grain brown rice
2 cups water
¼ cup olive oil
1 teaspoon soy sauce
2 tablespoons lemon juice
pepper to taste
1 green onion, minced
1 tablespoon parsley, minced

Bring the rice and water to a boil and simmer until fluffy, about 45 minutes. Set aside and cool completely. In a small bowl, whisk together the olive oil, soy sauce, lemon juice and pepper. Pour this liquid over the cooled rice. Top with minced green onion and parsley and toss until completely mixed. Chill 1 hour and serve.

Serves 4.

Nutty Tropical Fruit Salad

2 bananas, chopped
½ cup crushed pineapple, drained
1 avocado, pared and diced
1 cup grapes
1½ cups cantaloupe
¼ cup dates, chopped
½ cup lime juice
¾ cup macadamia nuts, chopped fine
½ cup coconut, shredded
⅛ teaspoon cardamon
½ cup mandarin orange slices, drained, to garnish

Combine everything except the garnish in a large bowl and toss gently but thoroughly until the flavors have mixed. Garnish top of salad with orange slices and serve.

Serves 8.

Sprouted Apples and Oranges Salad

4 ounces alfalfa sprouts
1 cup iceberg lettuce, shredded
1 cup Romaine lettuce, shredded
¼ cup parsley, minced
¼ cup green onion, minced
1 cup celery, diagonally sliced
½ cup water chestnuts, patted dry and sliced
1 cup mandarin oranges, drained
⅓ cup safflower oil
2 tablespoons lemon juice
1 tablespoon herbed white vinegar
1 teaspoon honey
¼ teaspoon pepper
½ teaspoon Dijon-style mustard
2 red apples, cored and cubed
½ cup raw cashews, finely chopped

In a large glass salad bowl, combine the sprouts, lettuces, parsley, onion, celery, water chestnuts and oranges. Do not toss, but cover and chill while you make the dressing. In a bowl whisk together the oil, lemon juice, vinegar, honey, pepper and mustard until smooth. Let stand at room temperature 20 minutes, then pour over salad ingredients. Add apples and cashews to all and toss well.

Serving Suggestion: Add two wedges of tangy cheese to this salad for a complete entree. Serve an iced herb tea for a luxurious presentation.

Serves 8.

Easy Bleu Cheese Dressing

4 ounces cream cheese
½ cup buttermilk
2 cups mayonnaise
2 ounces Bleu cheese
¼ teaspoon garlic powder
2 drops Tabasco sauce

Soften the cream cheese at room temperature, then whip until smooth. Stir in buttermilk and mayonnaise until fluffy, then crumble in Bleu cheese, garlic powder and Tabasco. Whip 1 minute, then cover and chill until served over tossed green salad.

Makes 3¼ cups.

Easy Dressing for Fruit Salad

1 cup honey
1 teaspoon Dijon-style mustard
1 teaspoon celery seed
1 teaspoon grated onion
¼ teaspoon salt
¼ cup lemon juice
¼ cup white vinegar
1 cup safflower oil

Combine honey with mustard, celery seed, onion, salt and lemon juice and whisk vigorously. Add in vinegar and continue to whip, then drizzle in oil and keep stirring 1 minute after oil is combined. Pour over mixed fruit salad. Store chilled.

Makes about 2½ cups dressing.

Easy, No-Cook Hollandaise

½ cup lemon juice
2 tablespoons Dijon-style mustard
4 egg yolks
1½ cups olive oil
pinch curry powder

In a glass bowl, whisk together the lemon juice and mustard. When smooth add in the egg yolks and whip until creamy. Slowly add in the olive oil, beating until all is included. Add in curry powder and whisk until well blended. Use on seafood, avocado salads and all other places this sauce is found. Perfect with steamed asparagus!

Makes 2½ cups.

Lime-Curry Dressing

½ cup olive oil
3 tablespoons lime juice
2 tablespoons honey
1 teaspoon lime zest, grated
1 teaspoon celery seed powder
½ teaspoon curry powder

Whisk all ingredients together until smooth. Excellent served over fruit, green or mixed vegetable salads. Also good with cottage cheese and fruit salads.

Makes 1 cup.

Feta-Herb Dressing

½ cup feta cheese, crumbled
¼ cup buttermilk
¼ cup plain yogurt
1 tablespoon lime juice
2 tablespoons parsley, or oregano, or chives, or tarragon, or combination

Combine all ingredients in a bowl or blender and whip until smooth. Particularly good served with spinach salad, and over sliced tomatoes and cottage cheese.

Makes 1 cup dressing.

A Dressing That's a Meal

This dressing is one after my own heart, since adding it to mixed greens produces a balanced meal. This makes enough for four large dinner or luncheon entrees. Combine Romaine, iceberg and Bibb lettuces and garnish with this dressing:

2 red radishes, minced
2 eggs, hard-boiled and chopped
1 garlic clove, mashed
1 tablespoon green pepper, minced
½ cup ricotta or cottage cheese
½ cup plain yogurt
½ teaspoon Dijon-style mustard
2 tablespoons lemon juice
½ teaspoon caraway seeds, crushed
½ teaspoon paprika
dash soy sauce
1 tablespoon black olives, minced

Combine everything together in a glass bowl and mix with a wooden spoon until smooth and light. Chill 1 hour before serving over assorted greens.

Makes 2 cups. Serves 4 salads.

Dill-Yogurt Dressing

½ cup plain yogurt
¼ cup safflower or olive oil
1 tablespoon fresh dill weed
  or
1 teaspoon dried dill weed
dash cayenne pepper

Combine all ingredients in a blender or bowl and whip until smooth.

Makes ¾ cup dressing.

Classic Vinaigrette

1 tablespoon shallots, minced
1 teaspoon Dijon-style mustard
2 tablespoons red wine vinegar
5 tablespoons olive oil
½ teaspoon soy sauce
fresh pepper to taste

In a small bowl combine the shallots, mustard and vinegar. Whisk until smooth, then add in oil and seasonings. Continue to whisk until well-blended. (Definitely mix the first three ingredients well before adding in the oil. Failure to do this will result in an oily-tasting dressing.)

This dressing will accent 1½ pounds of steamed and chilled broccoli, Brussels sprouts, wilted salad or cauliflower. Pour over chilled vegetables and serve immediately. Do not return this combination to the refrigerator as the dressing will separate and harden.

Makes ½ cup.

Fresh Spinach Dressing

1 cup spinach leaves, packed
2 green onions, chopped
⅛ teaspoon tarragon
¼ cup safflower oil
1 tablespoon lemon juice
2 tablespoons apple cider vinegar
1 teaspoon honey
dash pepper

Whirl all ingredients together in a blender until perfectly smooth. Store chilled until served.

Variation: This may be changed by the addition of 2 tablespoons sesame tahini and a dash of garlic powder or fresh garlic clove.

Makes about 1 cup.

Creamy Russian Dressing

½ cup cucumber, peeled, seeded and chopped
1 green onion, chopped
½ cup tomato, peeled, seeded and chopped
¼ teaspoon cumin seed
1½ cups plain yogurt
1 teaspoon honey
pepper to taste

In a blender, puree the cucumber, onion, tomato and cumin together. Add in plain yogurt, honey and pepper and whip until smooth. Chill 1 hour before using. This dressing goes well with green salads, and also as a taco salad dressing.

Makes 2 cups.

Zesty Tahini Dressing

1 cup sesame tahini
½ cup water
½ cup lime juice
1 tablespoon orange juice
2 tablespoons lemon juice
3 tablespoons soy sauce
1 garlic clove, bruised
¼ teaspoon sesame oil
1 tablespoon parsley, chopped

In a blender, combine the tahini, water and juices. Whirl until smooth, then add in the soy sauce, garlic and sesame oil. When smooth, add in parsley and run only long enough to disburse parsley in dressing, as if it were very finely minced. Chill, covered until used. Before dressing a salad, allow to come to room temperature for full flavor benefit.

Makes 2½ cups.

Garden-Lush Cucumber Dressing

This dressing is perfect on any green salad, and is especially good served over more cucumbers. For the most cucumbery salad of all pour this dressing over 2 large peeled and sliced cucumbers and serve immediately.

½ cup cucumber flesh, seeds removed
½ cup plain yogurt
1 garlic clove, bruised
2 tablespoons olive oil
1 teaspoon parsley, minced
¼ teaspoon dill weed
milk to thin (optional)

Combine all ingredients in a blender and whip until totally smooth and creamy. Correct seasonings with salt and pepper to taste if necessary. Add in milk, a teaspoonful at a time if you prefer a slightly thinner dressing. Chill 1 hour before using this dressing. Will dress 2 large cucumbers.

Makes about 1¼ cups.

MAIN DISHES
Fish, Meat, Vegetable

Oysters Rockefeller Divine

1 pound spinach, cooked and drained
1 shallot, finely minced
1 small garlic clove, minced
6 green onions, trimmed and minced
2 celery stalks, chopped
½ cup parsley, chopped
10 Bibb lettuce leaves, torn
2 cubes butter, melted
1 cup bread crumbs
1 tablespoon Worcestershire sauce
1 tablespoon anchovy paste
3 drops Tabasco sauce
2 dozen oysters on the half shell
¼ cup dry sherry
½ cup bread crumbs
¾ cup Parmesan cheese

Combine first 8 ingredients in blender until smooth. Add in bread crumbs, Worcestershire sauce, anchovy paste and Tabasco and whirl until mixed well. Remove oysters with a bit of sherry, scrub shells and set aside. Simmer oysters with sherry just to the boiling point. Place an oyster in each shell, and divide the sauce among the oysters. Mix the breadcrumbs and cheese and garnish oysters. Bake at 450 for about 8-10 minutes. Serve immediately.

Serves 4.

Shrimp Jambalaya

1 cup short grain brown rice
2 cups water
1 teaspoon sea salt
1½ pounds cooked shrimp
5 tablespoons butter
1 tablespoon olive oil
1 cup onions, sliced
3 garlic cloves, pressed
1 pound can of tomatoes, with juice
3 tablespoons tomato paste
¾ cup celery, diagonally sliced
½ cup green pepper, chopped
1 cup peas
1 tablespoon parsley, minced
⅛ teaspoon cloves
½ teaspoon thyme
½ teaspoon cayenne pepper
¼ teaspoon black pepper

Bring water and rice to a boil, add in salt. Cover and simmer 20-30 minutes. When water is absorbed, fluff with a fork and set aside, covered. Saute the shrimp in oil and butter, along with the onion, and garlic. When onion is tender, add in remaining ingredients and simmer until liquid is reduced considerably. When mixture can hold its shape in a large spoon, add in rice, cover and simmer until liquid is absorbed. Serve directly from the cooking pot at the table.

Serves 6.

Handy Hint: Store no fresh or perishable food above the refrigerator or stove. The generated heat will turn the foods stale very quickly.

Salmon Brunch Puffs

These are perfect for a brunch entree or a first course for a more formal dinner.

1 cup water
½ cup butter
pinch pepper
1 cup whole wheat pastry flour
4 eggs, room temperature
¾ cup Swiss cheese, shredded
2½ cups salmon, chilled and flaked
¾ cup black olives, chopped
¼ cup celery, minced
1 teaspoon shallots, minced
½ cup mayonnaise
¼ cup plain yogurt
1 teaspoon curry powder
2 teaspoons parsley, minced

Combine the water and butter in a saucepan and bring to a boil. Add in the pepper and flour all at once and stir until a ball is formed, about 1 minute. Let it rest and cool for about half a minute. With an electric mixer, beat in the eggs, one at a time until the dough is dull and satiny each time. Finally add in the cheese and mix until smooth. Butter and flour a baking sheet. Drop dough by large tablespoons onto the sheet, 2" apart. Bake at 375 for 30-35 minutes. Cool on a wire rack, slitting the sides horizontally to allow steam to escape. Meanwhile, combine the salmon filling ingredients together in a glass bowl and mix completely. Chill, covered. Fill cooled pastry shells just prior to serving.

Serves 6.

Sole in Mushroom Sauce

6 sole fillets, large
pinch salt
1½ cups water
2 tablespoons white wine
1 onion, sliced in thin rings
4 tablespoons butter
2 teaspoons olive oil
½ pound mushrooms, sliced
2 tablespoons whole wheat pastry flour
½ cup sour cream or plain yogurt
½ teaspoon soy sauce
pepper to taste
6 cups fettuccini, cooked
2 tablespoons butter
1 tablespoon parsley, minced

Poach sole fillets in salted water. Add in white wine and simmer until tender. Remove fish and place in buttered baking dish. Reserve liquid. Saute onion in butter and olive oil until tender, then add in sliced mushrooms and cook 3 minutes. Add in flour and mix in well. Add poaching liquid back in and simmer until thickened. Cool 5 minutes, then add in sour cream, soy sauce and pepper. Pour over fish and bake at 350 for 10 minutes. Meanwhile, toss hot fettuccini with butter and parsley. Serve baked sole over fettuccini, being generous with the accompanying sauce.

Serves 6.

Handy Hint: When buying fresh, whole fish, check that the eyes are clear. A cloudy fish eye shows age.

Pilgrim Souffle

1½ pounds white fish,
    such as snapper, sole, halibut
2 tablespoons butter
3 tablespoons parsley, minced
½ cup celery, minced
½ cup onion, minced
3 cups whole wheat bread crumbs
4 cups milk
4 eggs, beaten
1 teaspoon salt
⅛ teaspoon mace
⅛ teaspoon pepper
2½ cups cheddar cheese, shredded
¼ cup black olives, chopped
¼ cup salsa (see index)

In a large skillet saute fish, parsley, onion and celery in butter until all are tender, about 10 minutes. (Fish will begin to break up into about 1" pieces.) Cover and set aside. In a large mixing bowl, combine the bread crumbs, milk, beaten eggs, seasonings, half the cheese and all of the olives. Mix thoroughly, then add in the fish mixture and stir well. Pour into a well-buttered 8 X 8 glass baking dish and top with the remaining cheese. Bake at 350 for 40 minutes or until it is lightly browned. Top with salsa and serve hot.

Serves 6.

Grilled Snapper with Curried Yogurt Sauce

½ cup mayonnaise
¼ cup plain yogurt
1 teaspoon parsley, minced
1 teaspoon dill weed
½ teaspoon curry powder
1 teaspoon honey
½ teaspoon soy sauce
2 pounds red snapper fillets
2 tablespoons butter

In a blender combine the mayonnaise, yogurt, parsley, dill weed, curry powder, honey and soy sauce and whip until smooth and fluffy. Set aside. Broil the snapper 10 minutes on a well-buttered pan, then turn and broil the other side. Remove and top with sauce, and return to the broiler to brown slightly. Serve hot.

Serves 6.

Handy Hint: For fool-proof cheese sauce, mix all ingredients in a blender before heating. No lumps, less stirring.

Shrimp Brazil

½ cup dried shrimp
1 cup water
2 onions, minced
3 garlic cloves, minced
2 tablespoons olive oil
2 large tomatoes, peeled, seeded and chopped
2 jalapeno peppers, minced
1 bay leaf
1 tablespoon ginger root, grated
1 teaspoon soy sauce
¼ teaspoon pepper
2 cups coconut milk, canned or frozen
2 cups water
2 tablespoons white wine
1 cup peanuts, ground
1 cup whole wheat bread crumbs
1 pound raw shrimp, cleaned
2 pounds white fish, in 1" chunks
2 cups long grain brown rice
5 cups water

Soak dried shrimp in warm water for 1 hour, then drain and puree in the blender. Saute onion and garlic in oil, then add tomatoes, seasonings, coconut milk, water and wine and cook 15 minutes. Add in shrimp and white fish, and cook until tender, about 10 minutes. Adjust consistency to thick cream with water or by rapidly heating to reduce moisture. Meanwhile, cook rice in water until tender, about 40 minutes. Serve together for a marvelous feast.

Serves 8.

Lamb and Vegetable Kebob Dinner

2 pounds lamb, cubed
15 medium mushrooms, cleaned
1 zucchini, thick sliced
15 cherry tomatoes, tops removed
2 green peppers, seeded and chunked
15 pineapple chunks
½ cup soy sauce
¼ cup green onion tops, minced
3 tablespoons rice wine vinegar
2 tablespoons Worcestershire sauce
2 tablespoons honey
2 tablespoons cilantro, minced
  (fresh coriander or Chinese parsley)
1½ tablespoons sesame oil
1 tablespoon ginger root, shredded
1 tablespoon garlic, minced
1 tablespoon hot pepper oil (see index)

Arrange lamb, mushrooms, zucchini, tomatoes, green pepper and pineapple on wooden or metal skewers. Combine remaining ingredients in a blender and whip until well mixed. Place kebobs in deep dish, pour marinade over all and chill, basting every half hour or so. About three hours later, broil or barbeque kebobs until tender. Reserve remaining sauce for passing at the table.

Serving suggestion: This dish goes well with rice. Extra sauce is excellent served over the rice. Garnish with lemon wedges.

Serves 6.

Vegetable Curry Pie

2 tablespoons safflower oil
½ cup sliced onion
2 leeks, white part julienne cut
2 stalks celery, diced
1 red bell pepper, chopped
3 carrots, peeled and diagonally sliced
1 clove garlic, bruised and pressed
1 cup broccoli, loosely chopped
1 cup zucchini, shredded
½ cup green peas
1 heaping tablespoon curry powder
pinch cayenne pepper
2 large tomatoes, peeled, seeded and chopped
¼ cup water
¼ cup cocktail vegetable juice
1 tablespoon dry sherry
1 teaspoon sea salt
1 tablespoon peanut butter
1 tablespoon sesame tahini
3 tablespoons plain yogurt

Heat cooking oil, then stir fry onion, leeks, celery, pepper, carrots and garlic together until the onion is transparent and the carrot is about half-cooked. Add in broccoli, zucchini, peas, curry and pepper and continue to cook over slightly decreased heat for 5 minutes. Add in tomatoes, liquids, salt, peanut butter, tahini and yogurt and mix well. Simmer 2 minutes, then cover and let cool 15 minutes. Chill overnight, covered. Next day, prepare crust and line 6 cup casserole with pastry. Fill with curried vegetable mixture and top with remaining pastry. Score pastry, and bake at 350 for 30 minutes, or until pastry is browned and filling is bubbly. Serve immediately.

(See Pastry for Vegetable Curry Pie.)

Pastry for Vegetable Curry Pie

2 cups whole wheat pastry flour
1 cube butter
1 teaspoon salt
¼ cup garbanzo bean flour
  or
¼ cup canned garbanzo beans, drained
1 tablespoon parsley, minced
¼ cup icy water

Combine pastry flour, butter, salt and garbanzo bean flour together until dough clings together. Knead briefly with the hands, wrap in waxed paper and chill 15 minutes. Divide dough and roll out on floured surface to accommodate your casserole dish. Make sure lid piece has 1" extra border for tucking. Bake as directed.

Serves 6.

Handy Hint: For fresh vegetables every time, always prepare them last. By the time everyone gets up to the table the veggies are perfectly done.

Party Pesto

2 cups fresh basil, firmly packed
2 cups fresh parsley, minced
1 cup pine nuts
1 cup Parmesan cheese, grated
10 garlic cloves, bruised
2 cups olive oil
1 teaspoon pepper
¼ cup olive oil

Combine basil, parsley, pine nuts, cheese, garlic and 2 cups oil in a blender or food processor and mix until almost pureed smooth. Add in pepper, whip 5 more seconds and store in a quart jar. Float ¼ cup oil over the top of the pesto to seal out air until ready to serve.

Makes 4 cups pesto.

Serve with 2½ pounds of prepared pasta and serve 8-10 people marvelously.

Oniony Omelet

1 red onion, cut into rings
¼ cup butter
¼ cup sour cream or plain yogurt
½ teaspoon dill weed
6 eggs
2 tablespoons water
pinch cream of tartar
4 tomato slices
1 tablespoon parsley, minced
¼ cup Parmesan cheese

Saute onion in heated butter until tender. Pour off extra butter into omelet pan. Add sour cream and dill weed to onion and stir without heat. Whip eggs together with water and cream of tartar. Heat oiled omelet pan and cook omelet until almost firm. Fill with onion mixture, fold sides of omelet toward center. Top with parsley and cheese. Place on serving platter and serve.

Serves 3.

Kraut Tofu Pie

1 9" double-crust pie recipe (see index)
4 cups sauerkraut
1 tablespoon melted butter
1 tablespoon molasses
½ cup water
½ cup onion, minced
½ cup bread crumbs
2 cups tofu, pressed and cubed
2 eggs, slightly beaten
½ teaspoon pepper
1 teaspoon soy sauce
½ teaspoon caraway seed, crushed
dash allspice

In a large bowl combine the sauerkraut, butter, molasses, water, onion and bread crumbs together and toss lightly. Press tofu to extract any excess water out of it, then cut in cubes and add to kraut mixture. Mix eggs, pepper, and other seasonings together and pour into kraut mixture. Toss well, then fill pastry lined deep-dish pie plate with mixture. Top with remaining pastry and bake at 425 for 35 minutes. Check to see that it is steaming before serving. Let cool 5 minutes before cutting.

Serves 6.

Handy Hint: A plate of raw vegetables and dip put out while preparing a meal will keep your family out of the way and eating their "salad" at the same time.

Savory Porcupines

1 tablespoon safflower oil
1 pound ground lamb (chicken or turkey)
¾ cup cracked wheat
½ cup onion, minced
1 garlic clove, pressed
1 teaspoon kelp powder
¼ cup parsley, minced
3 tablespoons walnuts, minced
1 cup miso stock
1½ cups sour cream
¼ pound mushrooms, sliced

Heat oil in frying pan. Combine ground meat, cracked wheat, onion, garlic, kelp powder, parsley and walnuts and form meatballs. Lightly saute in oil, until browned. Cover with miso and simmer 25 minutes, covered. At the end, add in sour cream and mushrooms and cover but remove from heat. Let stand 5 minutes, then stir and serve.

Serving suggestion: Excellent served with hot rice or noodles.

Serves 4.

Chicken Donburi (Chicken with Rice)

½ pound chicken breast, cubed
8 mushrooms, sliced
2 tablespoons orange juice
2 green onions, julienne cut
½ cup bamboo shoots, sliced
½ cup soy sauce
¾ cup miso stock
½ cup Sake, or dry sherry
4 eggs, slightly beaten
4 cups cooked rice, heated

Pat dry chicken pieces and set aside. Soak sliced mushrooms in orange juice 10 minutes. Add chicken, mushrooms, onions, bamboo shoots and soy sauce to frying pan. Heat, adding in miso and Sake. Bring to a boil and simmer 5 minutes. Stir in eggs, reboil and remove from heat. Serve over rice, which has been divided into 4 large soup bowls. Serve immediately.

Serving suggestion: This easy entree is delicious with green tea and a cucumber salad side dish. See Index.

Variation: This dish is also successful served over vermicelli.

Serves 4.

Handy Hint: Any fruit stain can be removed by pouring boiling water through the affected material. If any stubborn stain remains, dab with hydrogen peroxide. Rinse and launder.

Sukiyaki (pronounced ski YA ki)

1 pound beef strips, sukiyaki cut
2 tablespoons honey
½ cup soy sauce
1 cup miso stock
1 teaspoon oyster sauce
1 cup bamboo shoots, sliced
6 green onions, julienne sliced in 3" pieces
2 dry onions, sliced
1½ cups yam noodles, cooked (clear noodles)
4 shiitake mushrooms,
  soaked, cleaned and sliced
3 celery stalks, diagonally sliced
¾ pound tofu, pressed and cut in 1" cubes
6 Nappa cabbage leaves, shredded
1½ cups long grain white rice
3½ cups water

Saute beef with honey until browned. Mix soy sauce, miso and oyster sauce in a bowl and set aside. Add bamboo shoots, onions and onion slices to skillet and saute briefly. Pour in sauce, add noodles, mushrooms, celery, tofu and cabbage and simmer, covered for 2-3 minutes, or until all vegetables are tender. Serve with boiled rice, made with rice and water listed, simmering 45 minutes.

Serves 6-7 generously.

Sour Cream Chicken Enchiladas

1 pound chicken breast, chopped
1 tablespoon safflower oil
1 onion, sliced
8-ounce can tomato sauce
1 tomato, peeled, seeded and chopped
1 teaspoon red wine vinegar
¼ teaspoon ground cumin
10-ounce can enchilada sauce
8-ounce can tomato sauce
½ pound undyed cheddar cheese, shredded
12 large corn tortillas
2 cups sour cream
1 cup black olives, chopped
1 green onion, minced

Saute chicken with oil, then add in onion and cook until all are tender. Add in 8 ounces tomato sauce, tomato, vinegar and cumin. Simmer 5 minutes and set aside. Combine enchilada sauce and 8 ounces tomato sauce in saucepan and heat to a boil. Set aside. Heat each tortilla in a dry griddle until flexible. Dip or brush with heated enchilada sauce, then fill with chicken mixture. Add in some sour cream and cheese and roll up. Place in baking dish. Repeat until all tortillas are used. Sprinkle with remaining grated cheese. Bake at 375 for 20 minutes, then remove and garnish with remaining sour cream and black olives, and green onions. Serve at once.

Serves 4.

Handy Hint: Remedy for drippy and smoking candles. Dip candles in soapsuds, then let dry before burning. Keep wick dry.

Baked Tofu

Tofu can be very ordinary by itself, but this baked entree, together with the barbeque sauce becomes very extraordinary. This is especially good used as sandwich "burgers," and offers a luscious alternative to ground meat. It also responds well to all the traditional garnishes you love.

2 pounds tofu
½ cup ketchup
2 tablespoons safflower oil
1 tablespoon red wine vinegar
¼ cup orange marmalade
1 tablespoon soy sauce
1 teaspoon garlic powder
1 teaspoon miso paste
½ teaspoon chili powder
½ teaspoon pepper
1 teaspoon Dijon-style mustard
½ teaspoon ground cumin
1 teaspoon coriander
1 teaspoon molasses
2 drops Tabasco sauce

Press tofu to extract excess water. Slice in ½" slices and place in buttered baking dish. Combine remaining ingredients in blender until smooth. Generously brush tofu slices with sauce. Hold reserve for dressing later, if needed. Bake at 325 for 30 minutes.

Note: This baked dish is also good served with toothpicks as a snack, and over rice as a complete main dish.

Makes 12-16.

Apple Millet Bake

1 large onion, sliced
1 green pepper, sliced
3 garlic cloves, bruised and pressed
1 cup eggplant, diced
2 baking apples, cored and sliced
¾ cup safflower oil
1 small can tomato paste
1¾ cups millet
4 cups apple juice
1 cup Romano cheese, shredded
1 cup cheddar cheese, shredded
1 tablespoon soy sauce

Saute the onion, green pepper, garlic, eggplant and apples in hot oil until all are tender. Add in tomato sauce, millet, apple juice and bake at 350 for 30 minutes. Cover tightly. Remove from oven and top with cheeses and soy sauce. Stir once to mix cheese into millet mixture. Bake uncovered another 15 minutes.

Serves 8.

Perfect Fondue

This fondue is great for bread or fruits, and can be a perfect centerpiece for a meal.

1¼ pounds Gruyere cheese, shredded
1 garlic clove, pressed
2 cups dry white wine
dash fresh nutmeg
dash white pepper
1 tablespoon potato flour
1 tablespoon Kirsch
extra wine to thin

Heat wine, then add in cheese, garlic, nutmeg and pepper. Stir until smooth. Combine potato flour with Kirsch and whisk in. When fondue has thickened, serve with bread cubes and fruit cubes. Keep fondue hot at the table. When it becomes too thick, thin with a splash of white wine.

Serves 4.

Greek Tofu Pie

1 9" single crust pie pastry (see index)
1½ cups tofu
1½ cups onion, minced
½ pound cheddar, grated
½ pound feta, crumbled
½ cup black olives, chopped
1½ cups spinach, cooked and chopped
1 egg
¼ cup milk

Prepare pie pastry and have it ready. Press moisture from tofu, then crumble into a bowl. Add in onion, cheddar and feta. Sprinkle in olives and spinach. Whisk egg and milk together and pour over all. Toss lightly to mix, then pour into pastry shell and bake at 350 for 30 minutes, or until it bubbles in the middle. Remove and cool 10 minutes before cutting.

Serves 6.

Tasty, Low-Calorie Quiche

Take the crust out of a quiche and really affect the calorie-count!

5 eggs
1½ cups milk
1 can (8 ounces) water chestnuts, drained and sliced
¼ cup green onion, minced
2 tablespoons parsley, minced
1 tablespoon celery, minced
¼ cup black olives, chopped
½ teaspoon tarragon
½ teaspoon basil
dash pepper
¾ cup Gruyere or Swiss cheese
1 tablespoon butter

Whip eggs and milk together until smooth. Add in chestnuts, onion, parsley, celery, olives and seasonings and mix well. Fold in cheese until wet. Butter a 9" quiche pan or 4-10 ounce individual ramekins and pour batter in. Bake at 375 for 35-45 minutes, or until quiche has puffed and browned.

Serves 4-6.

Mexican Dinner Crepes

1½ cups whole wheat pastry flour
½ teaspoon sea salt
1½ cups milk
3 large eggs
dash nutmeg
2 tablespoons water
oil for frying
1 onion, chopped
1 tablespoon butter
2 cups spinach, cooked and drained
1 teaspoon soy sauce
2 cups sour cream
½ pound mild cheddar cheese, shredded
pepper to taste
1 onion, minced
1 tablespoon safflower oil
16-ounce can whole tomatoes, drained
4-ounce can green chilis, seeded
1 teaspoon salt
1 tablespoon white vinegar

Combine flour, salt, milk, eggs, nutmeg and water together in the blender until smooth. Let stand 5 minutes, then fry about ¼ cup batter at a time in an oiled 6" frying pan. Turn once to brown. Saute the onion in butter, then add spinach and soy sauce and simmer until tender. Fill the crepes with the spinach filling and place in baking dish. Top with sour cream, cheese and pepper. Bake at 350 for 30 minutes. Saute onion in oil until tender, then add in tomatoes, chopping well. Include chilis, diced, and salt and vinegar. Cook until boiling, then simmer 10 minutes. When crepes are taken from the oven serve this with "salsa."

Serves 6.

Snappy Tamale Casserole

⅓ cup olive oil
1¼ cups onion, chopped
1 cup whole kernel corn
¼ cup green pepper, minced
1 garlic clove, minced
1 cup tomatoes, peeled, seeded and chopped
¾ cup stone-ground corn meal
⅓ cup black olives, chopped
1 teaspoon sea salt
1 cup milk
2 eggs, beaten
1½ cups cheddar cheese, shredded
1 avocado, mashed
¼ cup sour cream

Saute onion in hot oil until tender, add in corn, green pepper, garlic and tomatoes and simmer 5 minutes. Stir in corn meal, olives, salt, milk and eggs and turn off the heat. Turn into a 6 cup casserole and top with cheese. Bake at 350 for 35-40 minutes. Remove and top with mashed avocado, then with sour cream. Serve immediately.
Serves 4.

Zucchini Pesto Trieste

⅓ cup fresh basil, packed
¼ cup olive oil
2 tablespoons pine nuts (may substitute walnuts)
¼ cup Parmesan, grated
2 garlic cloves, bruised
1 tablespoon olive oil
1¼ pounds zucchini
   (about 4 medium), julienne cut
1 teaspoon soy sauce
⅛ teaspoon black pepper
2 pounds pasta
water

Combine basil, oil, nuts, cheese and garlic in a blender or food processor and puree until smooth. In the meantime, heat 1 tablespoon oil in a frying pan and stir-fry zucchini until crisp, about 3 minutes. Season with soy sauce and pepper, then add in basil mixture and heat completely to simmer. Serve over pasta cooked al dente in adequate boiling water.

Simplicity Souffle

4 tablespoons butter
¼ cup whole wheat pastry flour
1¼ cups milk, warmed
5 egg yolks, room temperature
½ cup Gruyere cheese, shredded
½ cup Tilset cheese, shredded
⅛ teaspoon mace
⅛ teaspoon white pepper
5 egg whites, room temperature
butter

Heat the butter and flour together in a saucepan, stirring constantly for about 2 minutes. Gradually add in the warmed milk and cook about 1 minute. In a small bowl whisk the egg yolks until yellow and fluffy, then slowly whisk them into the warm milk mixture. Add in the two cheeses and seasonings and stir until all are melted completely. Set aside and cool to room temperature. Beat the egg whites until fluffy but not dry. Fold ⅓ of them into the cooled cheese mixture, then include the remaining egg whites. Gently pour the mixture into a well-buttered 6 cup souffle dish and ease it into the oven at 375. Bake for 30 minutes, then serve immediately.

Serves 6.

Savory Stuffed Peppers

4 green peppers, topped and seeded
3 tablespoons safflower oil
2 tablespoons celery
½ cup onion, chopped
½ cup long grain brown rice, cooked
1½ cups tofu, pressed and cubed
6 mushrooms, sliced
½ cup cheddar cheese, shredded
1 teaspoon parsley, minced
1 garlic clove, bruised and pressed
8-ounce can tomato sauce
soy sauce and pepper to taste

Drop the peppers into boiling water and cook for 5 minutes. Remove and completely rinse in cold water until cooled. Heat oil in a frying pan and saute celery, onion, rice, tofu, and mushrooms until tender. Add in cheese, parsley, garlic and tomato sauce and heat to simmering. Add soy sauce and pepper to taste, then continue simmering until mixture binds well and holds up in a spoon by itself. Stuff peppers with mixture and bake at 375 for about 45 minutes or until peppers are tender.

Note: Depending upon the size of your peppers, you may have enough stuffing for a 5th pepper.

Serves 4.

Jalapeno Hom Bow

1 cup warm water
1 tablespoon honey
1½ teaspoons yeast
3 cups unbleached flour
1 tablespoon butter, melted
1¼ cups kidney beans, cooked
2 tablespoons safflower oil
1 tablespoon onion, minced
1 tablespoon jalapeno chili, minced
½ teaspoon chili powder
3 tablespoons black olives, minced
¼ teaspoon soy sauce
¾ cup cheddar cheese, shredded

In a warm bowl, combine warm water, honey and yeast and allow to rest 10 minutes. Add in flour and melted butter and mix to form a dough. Knead 5 minutes on a floured surface, then allow to raise until dough is double in bulk in an oiled bowl, covered. Remove and knead 1 minute, then cut dough in half to make two long dough logs. Cut each in 12 equal pieces. Cover and let rise 5 minutes, then roll them out to 3" rounds, one at a time, fill with 1 tablespoon filling and close dough as shown in drawings. Make sure to pleat and pinch the top. Line a bamboo strainer with cooking parchment, then punch holes to allow the steam through. Steam hom bow in small groups for 10 minutes, until double in size. Serve immediately.

Filling: Saute beans in oil, together with onions and jalapeno. Mash until smooth, then add in chili powder, olives, soy sauce and cheddar and mix until smooth. Remove and cool before filling dough. Makes about 2 cups filling. (Note: This filling, doubled, is an excellent hot bean dip for the very brave.)

Makes 24.

1. Add filling. *2. Close dough around filling.* *3. Pleat and pinch at top.*

SIDE DISHES

Plain Old Baked Beans

Not so plain, really, these beans are a staple at every picnic. Admit it, you'd eat them more often if they were around. This recipe will make it easy to do that.

2 cups dry navy or pinto beans
water
1 green apple, cored and chopped
½ cup crushed pineapple
1 large onion, sliced
¼ cup molasses
3 tablespoons honey
2 teaspoons sea salt
2 tablespoons Dijon-style mustard
1 teaspoon miso paste

Wash beans, then soak in up to 8 cups water overnight. Wash again, then cover with water and bring to a boil, simmering 1 hour. Turn off heat, and add apple, pineapple, onion and molasses to beans. Stir well, then add in remaining ingredients. Pour into covered casserole dish, leaving 1" headroom at least. Add additional water if beans are not immersed in liquid. Bake at 300 for 5-6 hours, adding extra water if beans become dry during baking. When beans are tender, remove lid and brown for 30 minutes before serving.

Note: For travel to a picnic, wrap hot casserole in newspaper, then a wool blanket and set in a box. Will stay warm up to 3 hours.

Serves 8.

Spinach Au Gratin

2 10-ounce frozen spinach
or
2 pounds spinach, cleaned and chopped
¾ cup milk
3 eggs
½ cup cheddar cheese, shredded
3 tablespoons onion, grated
½ teaspoon soy sauce
dash pepper
¼ cup cheddar cheese, shredded
1 cup whole wheat bread crumbs
1 tablespoon butter, melted

Steam spinach until tender, then drain and pat dry. In a bowl, whip milk and eggs until frothy. Add in cooled spinach, together with cheese, onion and seasonings. Mix well, then pour into buttered 8 X 8" pan. Bake at 350 for 25 minutes. With a fork, combine cheese, bread crumbs and melted butter until well mixed. Top spinach with it, and return to the oven another 10-15 minutes, or until center is firm. Remove and let stand 5 minutes before serving.

Serves 6.

Handy Hint: Can't tell if an egg is raw or hard-boiled? Twirl it on the counter. If it spins, it's cooked. If it wobbles, it's raw.

Brooklyn Potato Pancakes

6 large potatoes, peeled
3 eggs, lightly beaten
¼ cup onion, grated
1 tablespoon unbleached flour
1 tablespoon whole wheat bread crumbs
1 teaspoon honey
1 teaspoon sea salt
dash pepper

Grate potatoes into cold water, then drain and pat dry. Mix eggs with all other ingredients, then add in potatoes and stir well. Pour by ¼ cup measure into oiled frying pan and spread mixture to 4" diameter. Fry until crispy and brown, then turn. Keep warm in oven until all are made.

Makes 18, serving 7-9.

Italian Polenta

3¾ cups water
1 cup cornmeal
½ teaspoon sea salt
½ cup Parmesan cheese, shredded

Bring 2 cups water to a boil. Combine remaining water with cornmeal and let soak until water is ready. Stir cornmeal mixture into boiling water, together with salt and cook, stirring frequently until thick. Cover and continue to simmer for 15 minutes. Add in cheese and stir well. Set aside and cool 30 minutes. Oil a 6-cup circular ring mold. Stir mixture well and pour in. Set in a pan of shallow water and bake at 350 for 30 minutes. Remove and invert over a serving platter. Fill with sauce or entree and serve immediately.

Serving Suggestion: Excellent with Shrimp Jambalaya (omit rice), Shrimp Brazil (omit rice) or pasta sauce. (See index)

Serves 6.

Salmon Croquettes Janna

1 cup brown rice, cooked
1 cup salmon, flaked and cooked
1 egg, beaten
1 teaspoon parsley, minced
1 egg, beaten
1 egg, beaten
½ cup whole wheat pastry flour
¼ cup safflower oil, for frying

With the hands combine rice, salmon, 1 egg, bread crumbs and parsley. Make 6 flat patties. Dip in beaten egg, then roll in flour and fry in hot oil in a frying pan until browned on both sides. Serve immediately.

Makes 6, serving 3.

Handy Hint: Love that pasta sauce but can't afford the calories? Use julienne-sliced zucchini and eggplant instead. Get the taste without all the extra calories.

Working Gourmet Quiche

For the diner who arrives tired, with 15 minutes before guests arrive.

4 eggs
1 cup milk
½ teaspoon cumin
½ teaspoon basil
1 green onion, chopped
1 teaspoon soy sauce
2½ cups cheese, grated (Gruyere preferred)
6-7 slices whole wheat bread
nutmeg to garnish

In a blender combine eggs, milk and seasonings. Pile cheese into quiche or pie plate lined with bread slices. Pour egg batter over all. Garnish with nutmeg and slide into 350 oven for 30 minutes. Cool slightly before cutting.

Serves 6.

Apple-Carrot Fritters

1 cup whole wheat pastry flour
1 cup milk
1 egg, beaten
½ teaspoon vanilla
½ cup green apple, shredded
½ cup carrot, shredded
dash cinnamon
dash nutmeg
oil for frying

Combine flour, milk and egg and whisk until smooth. Add in vanilla, apple, carrot and spices and stir until mixed. Drop by tablespoons into hot oil and fry until golden. Drain, then serve with butter.

Makes 36.

Swiss Potato Bake

¼ cup butter
1 large onion, sliced thinly
7 potatoes, peeled and sliced thinly
1½ cups Swiss cheese
¾ cup ricotta
1½ cups half and half
2 tablespoons honey
1 tablespoon parsley, minced

Butter a large casserole with half the butter, then layer in half the onion, potatoes, cheeses and ricotta. Repeat the process, then dot with the butter. Pour half and half, together with honey over all. Bake, covered at 350 for 1½ hours, then uncover and bake until browned. Garnish with parsley and serve.

Serves 10.

Handy Hint: Cheese can be easily frozen for later use, but it can be crumbly. To avoid this, let cheese defrost in the refrigerator for three days before eating.

Salsa Casserole

12 large tomatoes, peeled and seeded
½ cup green pepper, minced
1 garlic clove, pressed
1 jalapeno, minced
½ cup onion, minced
1 tablespoon olive oil
soy sauce and pepper to taste
3 cups whole wheat bread crumbs
1 cup cheddar cheese, grated

Chop tomatoes in a pie plate to reserve juice. Combine green pepper, garlic, jalapeno, onion and oil and saute until tender. Season, then add to tomatoes. Fold bread crumbs into tomato mixture, adding water or tomato juice if bread is not moist. Pour into buttered baking dish, top with cheese and bake at 350 for 25 minutes, or until mixture is the texture of stuffing.

Serves 8-10.

Handy Hint: To save energy, bake your turkey unstuffed. Use drippings from the half-baked bird to make the dressing and bake the dressing the last 45 minutes of the time.

Carrots in Cider

4 cups carrots, diagonally sliced
1¼ cups cider
1 tablespoon butter
½ teaspoon molasses
1 teaspoon orange peel, grated
1 teaspoon lemon peel, grated
1 tablespoon lemon juice
1 tablespoon sesame seeds

Combine carrots and cider and simmer, covered until tender. Add in butter, molasses and seasonings and boil rapidly to reduce the liquid to a syrup. Sprinkle with sesame seeds, toss and serve.

Serves 6.

Fried Rice

3 tablespoons safflower oil
3 cups brown rice, cooked
¾ cups onion, minced
1 cup mushrooms, chopped
1 tablespoon soy sauce
½ teaspoon garlic powder
1 egg
1 green onion, minced
1 tablespoon sesame seeds

Heat oil, then saute rice, onion and mushrooms until onion is tender. Add in soy sauce and garlic powder and toss lightly. Beat egg well, then fry in one side of frying pan until brown, then turn and brown. Remove from the pan and julienne cut. Return to rice mixture. Garnish with green onion and sesame seeds, toss lightly and serve.

Serves 6.

Sunday Morning Omelet

3 eggs
3 tablespoons water
1 teaspoon Parmesan cheese
1 teaspoon oil
6 peach slices, cooked
dash cinnamon
dash nutmeg
1 tablespoon honey
2 tablespoons sour cream
1 teaspoon walnuts, ground
1 tablespoon strawberry syrup or jam

Whip together the eggs and water until frothy. Heat oil and cheese in 10" frying pan until cheese browns. Pour in eggs and heat until almost done in the middle. Bake in preheated 400 oven for 3-5 minutes, to allow eggs to puff. Remove and top with filling in order listed, then fold over, put back in oven for 3 more minutes and serve.

Serves one very large omelet, which can serve two people.

Vegetable Tempura

This basic tempura batter is perfect for vegetables as well as fish. Keep your batter and ingredients cool and patted as dry as possible. If you have trouble getting the batter to stick, dust items with flour before dipping. Keep oil uniformly hot, and keep cooked foods warm in the oven, uncovered, until serving time.

1 cup ice cold water
1 egg
1 cup whole wheat pastry flour
about 2 pounds vegetables, including broccoli, zucchini, eggplant, parsley, carrot, green pepper, sweet potato, parsnip and green beans
oil for frying

Whip egg and water together until frothy. Stir in flour until almost smooth. Have vegetables ready, and heat oil to just over 375. Dip vegetables in batter, then into hot oil and fry until crispy.

Serves 4-6.

Handy Hint: If egg whites are stubborn and will not whip well, add in a pinch of baking soda and whip again.

Trusty Timbale

This light dish, almost quiche without the crust, is great baked in a large pan or in individual ramekins. Easy, and impressive, either way.

¼ cup butter
2 tablespoons whole wheat pastry flour
2 cups milk
1¾ cups cheese, grated
½ cup carrot, shredded
¼ teaspoon nutmeg
1 tablespoon orange juice or orange liqueur
1 teaspoon soy sauce
dash cayenne
8-9 eggs
1 tablespoon green onion, minced

Combine butter and flour and heat until browned. Whisk in milk and cook until smooth. Remove from heat and stir in cheese, carrots and seasonings. Beat eggs separately, then whisk them into the carrot batter. Pour into 6 individual ramekins, garnish with onion and bake at 350 for 30 minutes, or until set and browned.

Variation: This recipe can easily become a brunch or dessert dish. Substitute peaches for carrot, honey for soy sauce, vanilla for cayenne, and omit the onion.

Serves 6.

Indian Dinner Pudding

This excellent side dish adds texture and interest to a buffet.

1½ cups corn meal
½ cup molasses
4 cups milk
¼ cup butter
1 teaspoon cinnamon
¼ teaspoon nutmeg
½ teaspoon vanilla
2 eggs, beaten
1 cup shredded carrot

Soak cornmeal in molasses and milk for 1 hour. Bring to a boil, stirring constantly and simmer 5 minutes. Add in butter and seasonings and stir well. Set aside. Combine eggs and carrot and slowly add to cornmeal mixture. Pour into buttered 8 cup casserole and bake at 275 for 2-2½ hours. Have a pan of warm water in the oven also. Remove and cool before serving.

Serves 10.

Excellent Egg Foo Yong

½ cup onion, chopped
½ cup celery, chopped
2 cups bean sprouts, washed and patted dry
1 small can tuna, packed in water and drained
1 tablespoon parsley, minced
6-8 eggs, beaten
soy sauce and pepper to taste
Dipping Sauce (see index)

Combine onion, celery, sprouts, tuna and parsley in a bowl and toss until tuna is flaked and all is well mixed. Stir in beaten eggs (use enough to cover but not be sloppy) and seasonings. Fry by ½ cupfuls in heated, oiled frying pan. Turn when browned, then serve with dipping sauce.

Makes about 12.

Easy Egg Rolls

2 eggs
2¾ cups water
2 cups whole wheat pastry flour
oil
¾ cup bean sprouts
¾ cup cabbage, shredded
½ cup water chestnuts
½ cup bamboo shoots
5 green onions, minced
¾ cup tofu
1 teaspoon ginger root, grated
½ teaspoon soy sauce
½ cup mushrooms, chopped
1 egg
oil for deep frying

Whip together eggs and water, then add flour and whisk until smooth. Fry in light oil in a 10" pan, as you would crepes, quickly rotating pan with batter and returning excess batter to the bowl. Fry on one side only, and stack browned side up. Combine beansprouts and next 8 ingredients in a bowl and stir well. Add a slight ¼ cup of this mixture to each egg crepe, and roll up. Immerse in hot oil and deep fry until crisp, about 4 minutes. Drain, then serve hot.

Makes 20-24.

Beet-Kraut Side Dish

4 cups raw beets, grated
1½ cups sauerkraut, drained
½ teaspoon sea salt
1 teaspoon honey
2 tablespoons lemon juice
1 tablespoon fresh horseradish, grated
pinch chervil

Combine beets, kraut, sea salt and honey and simmer slowly in the top of a double boiler for about 1 hour, until beets are tender. In a small bowl combine the lemon juice, horseradish and chervil, then add to beet mixture, mix and steam 5 minutes on lowest heat. Stir and serve.

Makes 6 servings.

Dilly Green Beans

2 dry quarts whole green beans
4 sprigs fresh dill
4 garlic cloves
1 teaspoon dried red pepper
2 cups water
4 cups apple cider vinegar
½ cup sea salt

Bring a large pot of water to a boil, then immerse cleaned beans into it. Cook 5 minutes, then remove and rinse with cold water until cool. Pack 4 pint jars with whole beans, standing them upright in the jar. Into each jar place a sprig of dill and a garlic clove. In a large saucepan combine pepper, water, vinegar and sea salt and bring to a boil. Simmer 5 minutes, then ladle into jars just to cover the beans. Seal, process in a hot water bath 5 minutes, let cool and store in the refrigerator for 2 weeks. Serve chilled on salads, as a side dish vegetable (chilled or lightly steamed prior to serving) and as a garnish to vegetable cocktail-based beverages.

Makes 4 pints.

Polish Potato Pancakes

1 egg
1 cup milk
½ cup raw potato, grated
½ cup sauerkraut, drained
½ cup whole wheat pastry flour
1 teaspoon sea salt
pepper to taste
¼ cup oil, for frying

Combine egg and milk and whip until frothy. Add in potato, kraut, flour and seasonings and mix well. Let stand 15 minutes, then drop by ¼ cup measure into lightly oiled pan. Fry until golden, then turn and repeat. Keep warm until all are cooked, then serve.

Makes about 10.

Saucy Stir-Fry Cucumbers

1 tablespoon garlic, minced
2 tablespoons safflower oil
5 large cucumbers, cut in 2" strips, pared and seeded
2 tablespoons honey
2 tablespoons soy sauce
1 teaspoon dry mustard
1½" of small hot red pepper
1 teaspoon ginger root, grated
dash black pepper
¼ cup apple cider vinegar

Saute garlic in oil until browned, then remove and discard garlic. Stir-fry cucumber in oil until tender, then add in everything except vinegar and cook 2 minutes. Remove with slotted spoon and cool in a glass bowl, covered. Add in vinegar, stir and chill, covered for 2 hours.

Serves 4.

Luscious Stuffed Tomatoes

1 tablespoon butter
2 teaspoons olive oil
¼ cup onions, minced
2 tablespoons celery, minced
1 garlic clove, bruised and pressed
½ cup mushrooms, sliced then chopped
2 tablespoons almonds, sliced
¾ cup brown rice, cooked
2 tablespoons sour cream
3 tablespoons Romano cheese, grated
1 tablespoon whole wheat bread crumbs
½ teaspoon soy sauce
½ teaspoon thyme
1 teaspoon parsley
4 large tomatoes, topped and scooped out
butter

Heat butter and oil in a frying pan, then saute onion, celery and garlic until tender. Add in mushrooms and almonds and continue to cook another minute or so. Remove from the heat and stir in the rice, sour cream and cheese. Sprinkle in bread crumbs and seasonings and stir well. Stuff tomatoes, dot with butter and bake in buttered dish at 350° for 25 minutes.

Serves 4.

Healthy Barbara's Green Potatoes

Spirulina is high-protein sea algae with a problem all its own: how to eat it in an appealing way. This recipe will get you started.

4 red potatoes, large
2 beets with tops
1 tablespoon spirulina
2 tablespoons butter

Clean potatoes, and cut into large bite-size pieces. Wash beets and cut, together with greens. Steam potatoes and beets until tender, pour into a bowl, then sprinkle with spirulina and allow butter to melt. Toss lightly to coat vegetables. Serve immediately.

Serves 4.

Sweet Potato-Apricot Bake

¼ cup butter
½ cup slivered almonds
¼ cup honey
2 cups sweet potatoes
10 apricots, pitted and halved
3 tablespoons lemon juice
1 tablespoon lemon rind
¼ cup Bourbon (optional)
    or
¼ cup apricot nectar
1 tablespoon butter

Butter an 8" × 8" glass baking dish, then sprinkle in ½ the almonds. Drizzle in ½ the honey onto the nuts. Alternately arrange the sweet potato slices and apricot halves, face down in the dish. Sprinkle in the lemon juice and rind and the rest of the nuts and honey. Sprinkle the Bourbon on top, dot with remaining butter and bake at 375° for 30-40 minutes, or until the liquid is thick and bubbly.

Serves 6-8.

Potatoes Anna

One of the most gorgeous side dishes to make and eat.

3 pounds potatoes, peeled
1 tablespoon butter
1 cube butter, clarified
sea salt and pepper to taste

Thinly slice the potatoes and pat dry to remove any excess starch. Butter baking pan generously (8" cast iron or glass), then arrange first layer of potatoes attractively. Brush on clarified butter and season. Continue to make potato layers until all are used up. Then, press firmly to exclude any excess air between slices. Top with remaining butter and bake at 425° for 40-50 minutes. Remove from oven, loosen sides from pan and invert over a serving platter. Cut like a pie and serve wedges.

Serves 6.

Handy Hint: For a fast soup, simply add fresh vegetables to cocktail vegetable juice and simmer. Excellent for using up leftovers.

Greek Cheese Pie

This very fast, very rich and very nutritious dish will delight you.

12 eggs, beaten
1 pound feta, patted dry
1 pound ricotta
1 teaspoon parsley, minced
2 cubes butter, melted and cooled
½ pound filo dough
1½ cubes butter, melted for brushing

Mix eggs together until thick and smooth. In another bowl, mix the cheeses, parsley and 2 cubes butter together. Add in the eggs and stir well. Line a deep 13" x 9" pan with filo dough, which has been painted with butter between the layers. Use 10 sheets of filo. Pour cheese mixture in, and top with another 10 buttered layers of filo. Do not crimp or cut, but simply allow the dough to lay as it falls. Bake in the oven at 350 for about 30 minutes, or until golden.

Serves 10.

Note: This is an excellent brunch dish also.

Zucchini Confetti

3 medium zucchini, trimmed
1 large carrot, peeled
1 teaspoon salt
1 tablespoon olive oil
1 tablespoon butter
1 green onion, minced

Shred the zucchini and carrot and mix together in a bowl. Sprinkle with the salt and toss lightly. Let stand 15 minutes, then place in colander and let drain 10 minutes. Press firmly to extract any excess moisture. Heat oil and butter together, let foam stop, then saute onion. Add in zucchini and carrot and stir fry until crisp and tender. Serve immediately.

Serves 4.

Turkey Pastrami Burrito

This treat is the result of some unlikely leftovers and a very hungry cook!

1 flour burrito, large
6 slices turkey pastrami
1 small avocado, mashed
3 slices tomato
1 wedge lime
½ cup mozzarella, shredded
1 tablespoon hot sauce

Heat flour burrito in dry skillet until warm only. Place on plate and layer with pastrami, mashed avocado and tomato slices. Squeeze lime juice over all. Top with cheese and hot sauce, then roll up. Bake 15 minutes at 300° (or microwave until cheese melts) then remove and eat.

Serves 1.

Handy Hint: Reduce the greasy taste in gravy with the addition of a few tablespoons of wine. Boil the gravy rapidly to reduce and to alleviate the alcohol smell.

New Boston Stuffed Cabbage Leaves

2 medium cabbages (outer leaves will be used)
1 pound tofu, pressed and patted dry
2 onions, minced
3 tablespoons butter
1 tablespoon tomato paste
¼ teaspoon cinnamon
1 cup boiling water
¼ cup short grain brown rice
1 tablespoon tomato paste

In a large pot, bring water to boil. Remove outer leaves from cabbage and parboil about 4-5 minutes. Drain in colander and rinse with cool water. Press tofu to remove water, then cut in ½" cubes. Set aside. Saute onion in heated butter, then add in tomato paste, cinnamon, water and rice. Simmer 15 minutes, add tofu and simmer another 15 minutes, covered. Carefully remove the tough center vein from the cabbage leaves, cutting leaves in half. When filling is no longer runny, fill each cabbage leaf with 1 tablespoon filling, and roll tightly, tucking edges in. Continue until all filling is used. Butter the large casserole, line with smaller cabbage leaves, and place rolls into casserole. Combine remaining tomato paste with enough water to cover the rolls in the casserole, then cover and bake at 350° for about 1 hour.

Serves 6-8.

Garden Gourmet Burrito

½ cup zucchini, sliced
½ cup mushrooms, sliced
¼ cup green onion, minced
½ cup tomatoes, peeled and seeded and chopped
1½ cups refried beans
1 cup prepared hot sauce (see index)
¾ cup grated cheese
1 cup avocado, mashed
½ cup sour cream
1 cup lettuce, shredded
8 flour tortillas (whole wheat, if possible)
butter

Steam together zucchini, mushrooms, onion and tomatoes. Heat beans in separate pan. Combine hot sauce, cheese, avocado, sour cream and lettuce and set aside. Heat tortillas in a dry skillet until warm. Divide vegetable combo, beans, and lettuce combo among tortillas. Place in buttered dish and heat 10 minutes in a 400° oven. Serve immediately.

Makes 8.

COOKIES
Cakes, Pies, Frostings

Grandmother's Pumpkin Pie (Farm Style)

2 cups cooked pumpkin, mashed
½ cup honey
1 tablespoon blackstrap molasses
3 eggs, lightly beaten
1 cup milk
1 cup heavy cream
½ teaspoon ginger
½ teaspoon nutmeg
¼ teaspoon mace
½ teaspoon cinnamon
¼ teaspoon kelp powder
¼ cup Brandy
1 9" unbaked pie crust (see index)

In a large bowl combine the pumpkin, honey, molasses and eggs. Whisk until completely smooth, then add in milk, cream and flavorings Beat 2 minutes. Pour pumpkin batter into unbaked pie shell and bake at 425 for 10 minutes, then reduce the heat to 350 for 40 minutes or until firm. Remove and cool, then serve with whipped cream if desired.

Serves 8.

Creme Patissiere (Cream Filling)

This classic French pastry filling is perfect between layers of a cake, in a puff pastry or eclair and as a cream pie filling.

1 egg, room temperature
3 egg yolks
3 tablespoons whole wheat pastry flour
3 tablespoons honey
1 cup whole milk
¼ teaspoon vanilla

With a wire whisk, beat together the egg, egg yolks and flour for 2 minutes at a hefty pace. Drizzle in the honey and continue to beat briskly. Add in the milk and vanilla and mix well, then heat over boiling water in a double boiler until thick. Stir constantly to prevent curdling and do not boil. Cool to room temperature and then use as desired. (Will fill 1 dozen puff pastries or eclairs. Double recipe for cream pie.)

Makes 2 cups.

Handy Hint: When making pies for the freezer, carve an initial which represents the filling in the top crust. You will recognize the pie of your choice easily.

Savannah Pecan Pie

This pecan pie is not quite so rich as you might expect. You can actually eat a whole piece without getting stuffed!

1 9" pie crust, unbaked (see index)
6 eggs, beaten
1 cup honey
1½ teaspoons vanilla
¼ cup butter, melted
1 cup milk
½ cup whole wheat pastry flour
1 cup pecan halves
1 cup whipping cream
dash cinnamon

Prepare pie crust and set aside. In a blender combine eggs, honey, vanilla, butter, milk and flour and whip 2 minutes on highest setting. Let stand 5 minutes, then whip again for another 30 seconds. Pour into unbaked crust, then top with pecan halves. Bake in the oven at 350 for 40 minutes, or until puffy. Remove and chill up to 4 hours, then whip cream and decorate pie with cream. Serve immediately.

Seves 8.

Queen of Hearts Cherry Tarts

1½ cups almonds, ground
2 sticks butter
2½ cups whole wheat pastry flour
½ cup honey
1 egg, beaten
1 teaspoon lemon peel, grated
1 teaspoon vanilla
1 cup strawberry jam
¾ cup apple juice
3 tablespoons honey
1 tablespoon cornstarch
2 tablespoons water
4 dry pints sweet cherries, pitted

Cream nuts and butter together, then cut in flour. Whisk honey, egg, lemon peel and vanilla together and add to flour mixture. Stir until a firm dough is formed. Divide among 2 9" springform pans, and press into the bottom and slightly up the sides. Bake at 350 for 10 minutes, then remove and cool completely. In a saucepan, heat together the jam, juice and honey until steaming. Mix the cornstarch with the water and whisk into the jam mixture. Cook until thick, stirring constantly. Add in the cherries and gently fold them in. Remove from the heat and stir twice more. Pour cherries evenly between the two pastry crusts, spreading them evenly. Chill until set, then serve.

Serves 12. Royally.

Chocolate Whipped Cream Frosting

1 cup semi-sweet chocolate chips
¼ cup honey
2 tablespoons water
pinch salt
2 cups whipping cream
½ teaspoon powdered instant coffee (not granules)

Place the chocolate, honey, water and salt together in a double boiler set upon boiling water. Cover until slightly melted, then stir until fully melted. Set aside until room temperature. In a chilled bowl whip the cream together with the coffee powder until firm. Add about 4 tablespoons whipped cream into the chocolate mixture and stir. Then add the chocolate into the whipped cream and fold until just mixed together. Frost cake in the normal fashion, then chill for 3 hours so frosting has a chance to set up. Serve thereafter.

Frosts a 3-layer cake.

Carob Nut Brownies

½ cup butter
½ cup honey
2 eggs
½ teaspoon sea salt
2 teaspoons vanilla
½ teaspoon cloves
¼ cup carob powder
¼ cup wheat germ
⅔ cup whole wheat pastry flour
2 tablespoons milk powder
1 teaspoon baking powder
½ cup sunflower seeds
½ cup peanuts, roasted and chopped

Cream butter and honey until fluffy. Beat in eggs, salt, vanilla and cloves. Combine all other dry ingredients together and fold into wet ingredients. Fold in seeds and nuts, and turn into an oiled 8 X 8" baking pan. Bake at 350 for 20-25 minutes. Cool and cut.

Makes 12 brownies.

Raw Apple Cake

One of the fastest and most flavorful autumn cakes you can make.

4 cups apples, shredded
¾ cup honey
½ cup butter
2 eggs, beaten
2 teaspoons vanilla
2 teaspoons cinnamon
1 teaspoon baking soda
½ teaspoon sea salt
2 cups whole wheat pastry flour

Core and shred apples, packing them into the measuring cup. Cream honey and butter, then whip in eggs. Fold in apples. Combine all dry ingredients, then add to wet ingredients. Stir well, then turn into buttered and floured 13 X 9" baking pan. Spread out in pan, then bake at 350 for 40-45 minutes, or until it springs back when touched in the center. Remove and cool. Frost (see index) and serve.

Makes 18 pieces.

Grandma's Brown Rim Cookies

This simple tea cookie satisfies that need for a little something sweet.

¾ cup butter
½ cup honey
½ teaspoon sea salt
1 teaspoon vanilla
¼ teaspoon nutmeg
2 eggs, beaten
2½ cups whole wheat pastry flour

Cream butter and honey until fluffy, then add in seasonings. Whip in eggs, then flour and mix well. Drop by teaspoonful onto an oiled baking sheet. Flatten with a fork or with a damp cloth over a glass. Bake at 375 for 8-10 minutes. Excellent shortbread taste.

Makes 3 dozen.

Easy Does It Spritz

1 cup butter
¾ cup honey
1 egg, beaten
1 teaspoon vanilla
½ cup ground almonds
½ teaspoon almond flavoring
dash sea salt
½ teaspoon baking powder
2½ cups whole wheat pastry flour

Cream butter with honey until fluffy. Add in egg, vanilla, almonds and seasonings. Combine baking powder with flour and add to wet ingredients. Mix well, then form into two dough logs and wrap in waxed paper. Chill 2 hours, then remove and cut. Bake on an oiled baking sheet at 375 for 7-8 minutes. Do not brown these cookies. You may wish to garnish them with a little red berry jelly after baking. Strawberry or currant are very traditional.

Makes about 8 dozen small cookies.

Coconut Shortbread

1 cup butter, room temperature
½ cup honey
1¾ cups whole wheat pastry flour
1 cup coconut, shredded fine

Combine all ingredients with your hands until you work them into a ball. Wrap and chill the ball for 1 hour. Roll the dough on a lightly floured surface to ½" thickness and cut into desired shapes. Bake at 300 for 10 minutes on an unoiled cookie sheet.

Makes 2 dozen.

Molasses Snaps

¾ cup butter
½ cup honey
¼ cup blackstrap molasses
1 egg
1 teaspoon lemon peel, grated
2 teaspoons baking soda
¼ teaspoon instant coffee powder
2 cups whole wheat pastry flour
½ teaspoon cloves
1 teaspoon ginger
1 teaspoon cinnamon
¼ teaspoon sea salt

Cream butter and honey until fluffy, then add in molasses, egg and lemon peel. Combine all dry ingredients together, then fold into wet ingredients completely. Cover and chill 2 hours or overnight. Form into 1" balls, then press flat with a powdered sugar coated glass bottom. Bake on an unoiled cookie sheet, placing dough 2" apart. Bake at 375 for 8-10 minutes.

Makes 4 dozen.

Natural German Carob Cake

¾ cup butter
¾ cup honey
4 eggs, separated
2 teaspoons vanilla
2 cups whole wheat pastry flour
¾ cup carob powder, sifted
½ tablespoon baking soda
1 teaspoon cinnamon
1 teaspoon cloves
1 teaspoon sea salt

Cream together butter and honey until fluffy. Add in egg yolks and vanilla and whip until light. Combine all dry ingredients and mix together well. Add to wet ingredients and mix well. Whip egg whites until firm and fold into batter. Pour batter into buttered and floured 13 X 9" pan and bake at 350 for about 30-35 minutes. Cake is done if it springs back when pressed lightly with a finger. Remove from oven and cool on wire rack. Frost with German Cake Frosting

German Cake Frosting

1 cup cream cheese
¼ cup honey
½ cup coconut, shredded
½ cup pecans, minced
1 teaspoon rum or rum flavoring
1 teaspoon orange rind, grated

Cream the honey and cream cheese together until fluffy. Mix in coconut, pecans and flavorings and stir well. Frost cake. Frosts a 2-layer cake.

Makes 2¼ cups frosting.

Heavenly Date Squares

2 cups old fashioned rolled oats
1 cup whole wheat pastry flour
½ teaspoon sea salt
½ lemon rind, grated
¼ cup safflower oil
¼ cup honey

Toss together the oats, flour and salt. Add in the lemon rind, oil and honey and mix well until the dough is crumbly and completely combined. Pat ⅔ of the dough into a buttered 9" baking pan. Add in the following filling:

Filling

1½ cups dates, pitted
  or
1¼ cups figs, chopped and ½ cup honey
1¼ cups water
3 tablespoons lemon juice
pinch sea salt
dash cinnamon

Simmer the dates in the water until very tender. Mash the fruit completely, adding in the lemon juice, salt and cinnamon. Spoon this directly onto the dough. Cover the filling with the remaining dough and pat it down firmly. Bake at 350 for 40 minutes. Cool slightly before cutting.

Variation: Rather than selecting between dates and figs, a half and half combination is also an excellent treat. (When using figs, you may wish to mash them in a blender after simmering.)

Makes 12 squares.

Veranda Orange Cookies

1 cup butter
1 cup honey
½ cup orange juice
2 eggs
1 teaspoon cinnamon
2½ tablespoons orange peel, grated
3 cups whole wheat pastry flour
1 teaspoon baking soda
1 teaspoon sea salt
1 teaspoon ginger
1 tablespoon vanilla

Cream together the butter and honey, drizzling in the honey slowly and beating the mixture until very fluffy. Mix in the orange juice, eggs, cinnamon and peel and whip lightly. Combine the dry ingredients, then add to the batter, mixing well. Finally, add in the vanilla and stir. Drop dough onto oiled cookie sheets and bake at 375 for 10 minutes. Cool on a wire rack before serving.

Makes 4 dozen 3" cookies.

Spicy Applesauce Squares

⅓ cup butter
¾ cup honey
1 cup applesauce, unsweetened
1½ cups whole wheat flour
⅓ cup soy flour
1 teaspoon baking soda
½ teaspoon sea salt
1 teaspoon cinnamon
2 teaspoons ginger
½ teaspoon cloves
1½ cups walnuts, chopped

Cream the butter and honey until smooth and fluffy. Fold in the applesauce. Sift the dry ingredients together, then stir them into the wet mixture. Fold the walnuts in, then pour the batter into an oiled and floured 8" square pan. Bake at 350 for 30 minutes. Cool on a wire rack, then frost (see index) and serve.

Makes 9 servings.

Fruit Smoothie Cheesecake

1½ cups graham cracker crumbs
2 tablespoons butter, melted
2 tablespoons honey, heated
1 pound tofu, drained
8 ounces cream cheese
2 eggs
½ cup honey
1 teaspoon lemon peel, grated
1 teaspoon vanilla
2 ripe bananas
¾ cup crushed pineapple, drained
¼ cup shredded coconut, unsweetened

Combine crumbs, butter and honey in a 9" pie plate. Remove 1 tablespoon for garnish. Press crumbs into sides and bottom of pie plate. Set aside. In a large bowl combine the tofu, cream cheese, eggs, honey, lemon peel and vanilla. Whip until blended. Add ½ of this mixture into the blender and whip until smooth. Add one banana and puree. Pour into a second bowl. Repeat with the remaining unblended mixture and fruits and fold in. Pour batter into the unbaked crust. Bake at 325 for 1 hour, then remove and cool. Garnish with the remaining crumbs. Chill 1 hour before serving.

Serves 10.

Handy Hint: For non-stick cookies, bake on kitchen parchment.

Banquet Kiwi Tarte

1½ cups walnuts, coarsely ground
1½ sticks butter
¼ cup honey
2½ cups whole wheat pastry flour
1 egg, beaten
½ teaspoon lemon peel, grated
½ teaspoon lime peel, grated
1 teaspoon vanilla
8 kiwi fruits, peeled and sliced
1½ teaspoons unflavored gelatin
3 tablespoons Brandy
⅓ cup apricot preserves

Combine walnuts with butter and honey and mix until crumbly. Add in flour and toss completely. Add in egg and flavorings and mix well until dough holds together. Butter a 14 X 10" pan and press the dough into the bottom and part way up the sides. Bake at 375 for 10 minutes. Remove and cool completely. Decoratively layer the sliced kiwi fruits in the cooled crust. In a saucepan combine the gelatin and Brandy and let stand 5 minutes. Heat slowly, adding in the preserves. Continue heating, but do not boil, until mixture is smooth. Remove and cool slightly, then generously brush the kiwi slices with the glaze, using it all. Chill, covered, until time to serve.

Serves 15.

Crown of Glory Custard Pie

8 ounces cream cheese
2 cups tofu, pressed and drained
⅓ cup lemon juice
½ cup butter, melted and cooled
⅔ cup honey
½ teaspoon sea salt
2 teaspoons vanilla
up to ¼ cup water, if needed
¼ teaspoon nutmeg
1½ cups graham cracker crumbs
¼ cup honey
¼ cup butter, melted
1 teaspoon cinnamon
1½ cups strawberries, mashed
1 tablespoon cornstarch
2 tablespoons water
3 tablespoons honey

Combine cream cheese, tofu, lemon juice, melted butter, honey, sea salt and vanilla in food processor or blender and whip until smooth. Only add in water if mixture is too thick to process. Mix in nutmeg and set aside. Combine graham cracker crumbs, honey, butter and cinnamon in a 9" pie plate, then press into the sides and bottom. Pour custard batter in and bake at 350 for 30-35 minutes, or until golden and puffy. Remove and cool. Meanwhile, combine strawberries, cornstarch dissolved in water, and honey in saucepan and cook until thickened. Cool completely. Top pie when both are cool, then chill until served.

Serves 12, as this is a very rich dessert.

Baked Coconut Cream Pie

1 9" unbaked pie shell (see index)
½ cup milk powder
1 cup water
2 eggs
2 tablespoons honey
½ teaspoon vanilla
1½ cups shredded coconut, unsweetened
1 cup whipping cream
1 teaspoon rum

Prepare pie shell. Preheat oven to 450. Whisk together milk powder and water (may want to use a blender), then add in eggs, honey and vanilla and mix until smooth. Add in coconut and stir. Pour into pie shell and bake at 450 for 10 minutes. Then lower temperature to 300 and bake for 30 minutes. Remove and cool to room temperature, then chill 1 hour. Whip cream together with rum until stiff peaks form. Top cooled pie and chill until served.

Serves 8.

Standard Graham Cracker Crust

1½ cups graham cracker crumbs
¼ cup honey
¼ cup butter
1 teaspoon cinnamon.

Combine all ingredients in a 9" pie plate. Use a fork for greatest success in mixing and disbursing. Press mixture into the sides and bottom of the plate. For unbaked fillings, fill unbaked crust with filling and bake according to filling instructions. For a cooked filling, bake crust at 375 for 10-12 minutes. Remove and cool, then fill with cooked filling. Garnish and serve as directed for filling recipe.

Makes 1 9" pie crust.

Standard Pie Pastry Crust

1½ cups whole wheat pastry flour
½ cup wheat germ, raw and untoasted
⅔ cup butter
pinch sea salt
up to ¼ cup icy water

Combine flour and wheat germ and toss lightly to mix. Cut in butter until consistancy of corn meal. Add in salt and toss lightly. Sprinkle in icy water, using only enough to get dough to stick together. Form a ball with the hands, then wrap in wax paper and chill 1 hour. Remove and let dough come to room temperature for 15 minutes. Roll out half the dough on a floured surface, shape into a pie plate. Repeat process with the other half of the dough, either topping the first pie, or lining a second pie plate. Fill crust according to directings for the filling involved, and bake accordingly. For a baked, empty crust, poke holes with a fork in sides and bottom and bake at 425 for 10 minutes. Remove and cool before filling with a cooked or chilled filling.

Note: when baking whole wheat crusts, do not wait for them to "brown." Since they start out brown as it is, "browning" usually is too done. This rule tends to apply to whole grain cookies also.

Makes 2 9" crusts, or 1 9" covered pie.

Fast One-Crust Pastry

1 cup whole wheat pastry flour
⅓ cup butter
pinch sea salt
pinch lemon peel, grated
2 tablespoons icy water

Cut flour and butter together with pastry cutter. Add in salt and lemon peel and toss, then sprinkle in water to form a firm ball of dough. Wrap in waxed paper and chill 30 minutes, then remove and roll on floured surface. Shape into a 9" pie plate, then fill and bake according to the filling instructions. For cooked filling, bake unfilled crust, after first poking holes in sides and bottom of crust with a fork, at 400 for 10 minutes. Cool and fill as required.

Makes 1 9" crust.

Best Cream Cheese Frosting

8 ounces cream cheese
¼ cup butter
2 teaspoons vanilla
1 teaspoon lemon peel, grated
1 cup milk powder, sifted

Cream the cheese with the butter, then add in the vanilla and lemon peel and whip 1 minute. Slowly add in the milk powder, until frosting is thick and spreadable. (May need a little more milk powder.) Whip 2 minutes for maximum fluffiness. Spread on cake or cupcakes.

Makes 2½ cups frosting.

Greek Torte

1 cup butter
¼ cup honey
3 egg yolks, beaten
1 teaspoon vanilla
½ teaspoon baking powder
¼ cup milk
¼ teaspoon lemon peel, shredded
1 jigger Brandy
3-3¾ cups whole wheat pastry flour
1 pound jar fruit preserves (honey-packed)
1 egg white, lightly beaten

Cream butter with honey until lightly fluffy. Add in beaten egg yolks and vanilla and whip. Sprinkle in baking powder, then pour in milk. Whisk vigorously, then include lemon peel and Brandy. Add the flour in a half cup at a time until a soft dough is formed. Knead 1 minute on a floured surface, then roll ⅔ of the dough out; enough to line a 10 X 14" shallow dish. Spread preserves inside the dough. Roll out the remaining dough and cut in 1" wide strips to form lattice-work over the preserves. Finish off the edges with crimping, and brush the dough with egg white. Bake at 350 for about 40 minutes, or until bubbly and golden. Remove and cool slightly before serving.

Serves 12.

Cascade Carrot Cake

1½ cups butter
1¼ cups honey
3 eggs
2 cups whole wheat pastry flour
1 teaspoon sea salt
1 teaspoon kelp powder
2 teaspoons baking soda
2 teaspoons cinnamon
pinch allspice
pinch mace
pinch nutmeg
3 cups carrot, grated
1½ cups walnuts, chopped
½ cup raisins, chopped
Cream Cheese Frosting (see index)

Cream butter and honey until light and fluffy. Whisk in eggs. Combine dry ingredients and toss lightly. Add carrot to egg mixture and fold in well. Pour dry ingredients into wet and stir well until all is wet. Add walnuts and raisins and stir briefly. Spread evenly in an oiled and floured 13 X 9" baking dish and bake at 300 for about 1 hour. Test for doneness with a toothpick. Remove and cool on a wire rack. Frost and serve.

Serves 15 generous pieces.

Mile High Strawberry Pie

1 baked 9" graham cracker crust (see index)
2 cups strawberries, mashed
1 envelope unflavored gelatin
½ cup honey
1 cup plain yogurt
1 tablespoon lemon juice
1 teaspoon vanilla
1 cup whipping cream
dash nutmeg

Place mashed berries and gelatin in a small saucepan. Let stand 5 minutes, then heat to boiling. Reduce heat and simmer 1 minute. Add in honey, stir and set aside to cool to room temperature. Chill until half set, then whisk in yogurt, lemon juice and vanilla. Chill another 15 minutes, then whip cream and fold it into berry mixture along with nutmeg. Pour all into the cooled crust and chill 4 hours before serving.

Serves 8.

Creamy Carob Frosting

3 tablespoons butter
¼ cup honey
⅔ cup powdered milk
2 tablespoons carob powder, sifted
3 tablespoons whipping cream
1 tablespoon frozen orange juice
1 teaspoon vanilla
dash cloves

Cream butter and honey until fluffy. Add in powdered milk and carob and whip well. Slowly add in whipping cream and orange juice, then flavor with vanilla and cloves. Whip 5 minutes for maximum fluffiness. Frost a 2 layer cake.

Makes 2½ cups frosting.

Dutch Poppy Seed Cake

½ cup orange juice, warmed
2 teaspoons yeast
¼ cup honey
¼ cup butter
1 egg, beaten
¾ cup currants
2 tablespoons wheat germ
1 teaspoon sea salt
1 teaspoon vanilla
2 cups whole wheat flour
1 cup poppy seeds
up to ½ cup unbleached flour
¼ cup honey
2 tablespoons lemon juice
1 teaspoon lemon peel, grated
1 teaspoon rum

Combine orange juice and yeast and let stand 10 minutes. Cream honey and butter until fluffy, then whisk in egg, currants, wheat germ, sea salt and vanilla. Add in juice mixture and stir. Add in flour and poppy seeds and stir well until a ball forms. Sprinkle unbleached flour upon the table and knead the batter lightly. Press dough into an oiled bundt pan or other pan of your choice. Cover and let rise until double in bulk. Bake at 375 for about 35-45 minutes, depending upon the pan selected and the thickness of the dough. Remove and cool. Meanwhile combine the honey, lemon juice and lemon peel in a shallow saute pan and bring to a boil, simmering until it thickens. Remove from the heat and add the rum. Cool partially, then pour over the cooled cake. Let the cake stand several hours before serving.

Serves 8.

Fast and Easy Struesel Tea Cake

2 tablespoons whole wheat pastry flour
2 tablespoons butter
3 tablespoons honey
1 teaspoon orange peel, grated
dash cinnamon
½ cup walnuts, chopped
2 tablespoons graham cracker crumbs
¼ cup butter
¼ cup honey
1 egg, beaten
⅔ cup buttermilk
1 teaspoon vanilla
¼ teaspoon sea salt
2 cups whole wheat pastry flour
1½ teaspoons vanilla
½ teaspoon cinnamon

With a fork mix together the first seven ingredients and set aside. Cream the butter and honey until fluffy, then whisk in the egg, buttermilk and vanilla. Combine the dry ingredients and add, stirring well. Pour this batter into an oiled 8" baking dish. Sprinkle the struesel topping on top, and bake at 350 for 20-25 minutes. Remove and cool slightly, then serve.

Serves 9.

Handy Hint: When buttering a fluted baking pan, use a brush and cover every nook and cranny. Removal of the finished product will be perfect.

Old Fashioned Farmhouse Donuts

¼ cup butter
⅓ cup honey
2 eggs, beaten
¾ cup buttermilk
¼ cup banana, mashed
1 tablespoon baking powder
½ teaspoon sea salt
½ teaspoon cinnamon
¼ teaspoon nutmeg
4 cups whole wheat flour
oil for deep frying

Cream butter and honey together until light and fluffy. Whisk in eggs, buttermilk and banana and beat until smooth. Combine dry ingredients together and add to wet mixture. Shape dough into a ball in the bowl, then cover and chill 1 hour. When chilled, roll out to ½" thickness on a floured surface and cut with a donut cutter or other appropriate cutter. Place on oiled baking pan until ready for frying. Deep fry in turn in medium-hot oil (preferably peanut oil) for about 2 minutes. Lift from the oil with a chopstick and drain. Frost if you wish. (See index for frosting)

Makes 24.

Handy Hint: For more plump cookies that hold their shape, chill the dough 30 minutes before baking.

Applesauce Health Donuts

1¼ cups warm water
1 tablespoon yeast
¼ cup honey
½ cup applesauce, unsweetened
2 cups whole wheat pastry flour
1 teaspoon sea salt
2-3 cups whole wheat flour
¼ cup butter, melted
1 tablespoon orange peel, grated
½ teaspoon cinnamon
¼ teaspoon nutmeg
½ teaspoon vanilla
2 tablespoons butter
2 tablespoons honey
1 tablespoon carob powder, sifted
1-2 tablespoons milk powder
¼ teaspoon maple flavoring
dash cloves

Dissolve yeast in warm water and honey for 15 minutes. Whisk in applesauce and whole wheat pastry flour. Add in salt, 1 cup of whole wheat flour, the melted butter and next four flavorings. Stir well, adding in remaining flour until a stiff ball is formed. Knead on a floured surface until dough is smooth and elastic. Let rise until double in bulk in an oiled, covered bowl. Punch down, and roll out to ⅝" thick. Cut with 3" ring or donut cutter. Place on oiled cookie sheets, cover and let rise to double in bulk. Bake at 400 for 12 minutes, then reduce heat to 350 and bake another 20-25 minutes. Remove and cool. Make a thin frosting with the remaining ingredients and dip donuts. Chill to set frosting, then serve.

Makes 24.

High Energy Hiking Cookies

1 cup honey
½ cup butter, melted
2 tablespoons orange juice
1 teaspoon lemon juice
¼ cup wheat germ
¼ cup whole wheat pastry flour
2 cups rolled oats
½ cup pecans
¾ cup coconut
½ cup ground almonds
½ cup ground cashews
¼ cup ground raisins
¼ cup apple juice (or grape juice)
½ teaspoon vanilla
½ teaspoon kelp powder
¼ teaspoon cinnamon

Combine all ingredients in a large bowl and mix with the hands until completely smooth. Line a 13" X 9" baking pan with kitchen parchment, then press dough into dish. Bake at 350 for 20-25 minutes. Remove and cool 5 minutes, then cut while still warm. Store lightly covered.

Serving suggestion: This cookie is so rich it can be served as a candy by cutting in smaller pieces and rolling in cocoa powder or coconut.

Makes 15 bars.

Old Fashioned Strawberry Honey Sauce

This recipe is perfect for most fruits, so top your ice cream, crepe or pound cake with the fruits of the season.

1⅔ cups mashed strawberries
⅓ cup honey
⅓ cup orange liqueur (may use orange juice)
3 tablespoons lemon juice
1 teaspoon orange peel, grated

Combine all ingredients together in a saucepan and boil, stirring constantly. Reduce heat to simmer and cook 3 minutes. Chill, covered until ready to serve.

Makes 1½ cups.

BREADS
Yeast, Quick, Cereals

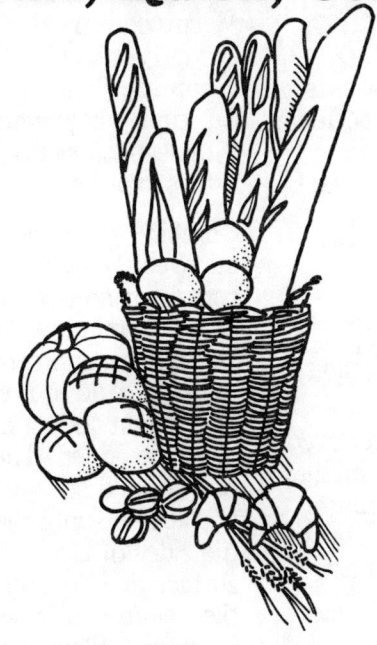

Old Country Pumpernickel

1 cup warm water
1 tablespoon yeast
¼ cup blackstrap molasses
½ teaspoon instant coffee
1 cup water
1 cup grated potato, raw
½ cup corn meal
2 teaspoons sea salt
2½ cups whole wheat flour
2½ cups rye flour
1 cup rye flakes
2-3 cups unbleached flour
1 tablespoon powdered cocoa

Combine warm water with yeast and molasses and let stand 15 minutes. Add in instant coffee, water, potato, corn meal, sea salt and whole wheat flour and stir well. Let stand 5 minutes, then continue by adding in rye flour and rye flakes, 1 cup unbleached flour and cocoa. Stir until ball forms in bowl, then turn out and knead with remaining flour until dough is smooth and elastic. When dough no longer accepts flour readily, oil hands and continue kneading dough with oiled hands for 5 more minutes. Let rise until double in bulk in an oiled and covered bowl. Punch down, knead 1 minute and form into 3 loaves. Place in oiled baking pans, and let rise, covered, until double in bulk. Bake at 350 for 45-50 minutes. Cool on their sides on wire racks, out of their pans.

Makes 3 loaves.

Crunchy Seven Grain Bread

This 6 loaf recipe is perfect for a giant batch of bread which is loaded with nutrition.

4 cups water
2 cups orange juice
½ cup honey
¼ cup yeast
¼ cup blackstrap molasses
½ cup safflower oil
3 cups oats
1 cup rolled barley
½ cup flax seed or meal
½ cup corn meal
1 cup rye flour
1 cup soy flour
5-7 cups whole wheat flour
1 tablespoon sea salt
1 teaspoon kelp powder

Combine water and orange juice with honey and stir well. Heat slightly to 100 degrees, then remove from heat and add yeast. Stir and let stand 15 minutes. Whisk in molasses, oil, oats, barley, flax and cornmeal and let stand 10 minutes. Add in rye and soy flours and stir well, then begin adding in whole wheat flour until 3 cups are added. Then add in sea salt and kelp powder and stir well. Continue adding in whole wheat flour until the dough comes away from the sides of the bowl. Pour dough onto a floured surface and continue to add flour by kneading the dough until a smooth and elastic ball of dough is formed. Place dough in an oiled bowl, cover and let rise until dough is double in bulk. Punch down, knead and shape into 6 loaves. Place in oiled pans, cover and let rise until double in bulk. Bake at 350 for 50 minutes, or until done. Oil crust for softer crust when slicing. Cool on their sides, out of the pans, on wire racks. Wrap and store.

Makes 6 loaves.

Scotch Rye Muffins

½ cup warm water
1 teaspoon yeast
½ cup orange juice
1 tablespoon molasses
2 tablespoons honey
2 tablespoons strawberry jelly
3 tablespoons safflower oil
¼ teaspoon sea salt
1 cup rye flour
¼ cup bran
½ cup oat flour
3 tablespoons whole wheat pastry flour

Combine water and yeast and let stand 10 minutes. Add in juice, molasses, honey, jelly and oil and whisk until smooth. Add in salt, flours and bran and stir well. Fill oiled muffin cups ⅔ full, let rise 10 minutes, and bake at 350 for 35 minutes. Remove from muffin tins to cool on wire racks.

Makes 1 dozen.

Lively Corn Bread

1 cup milk
¼ cup plain yogurt
1 egg, beaten
¼ cup butter, melted
2 tablespoons honey
2 tablespoons orange juice
1 cup whole wheat pastry flour
1 cup cornmeal
½ teaspoon sea salt
1 heaping tablespoon baking powder

Whip all wet ingredients together until smooth. Add in dry ingredients and blend only until all ingredients are wet. Spread into a buttered and floured 9" square baking dish and bake at 425 for 25 minutes. Serve this hot from the oven with butter and jam.

Makes 9 servings.

Pikelets
(sometimes called English Crumpets)

This recipe was shared with me by a favorite English family I know. It's about as authentic as I can get!

1¼ cups whole wheat pastry flour
½ teaspoon sea salt
1½ teaspoons dry yeast
1 teaspoon honey
½ cup milk, room temperature
½ cup water, warm
pinch baking soda

Combine the flour with the salt and set aside. Combine the yeast, honey and milk, then add in the warm water. Mix the dry and wet ingredients stirring until batter is soft. Cover and let rise 45 minutes. Dissolve the baking soda in 1 tablespoon water and beat into the batter. Let rise again for about 30 minutes. Oil a hot griddle, and oil 4" crumpet rings. Place rings on the griddle and ladle batter into them. Cook until the top of the batter is bubbled and set, then turn and cook the underside. Serve hot with butter.

Serving Suggestions: Crumpets are excellent served with ricotta cheese-honey-slivered almonds, warm jam, ricotta cheese-apple butter or other such combinations, not to mention butter and fresh strawberries. Perfect for breakfast, and of course, teatime.

Makes 8-10.

Sunrise Pineapple Pancakes

2 eggs, lightly beaten
1 cup milk
½ cup pineapple juice
1 tablespoon honey
2 tablespoons butter, melted
2 tablespoons safflower oil
½ cup crushed pineapple, drained
1⅞ cups whole wheat pastry flour
½ teaspoon sea salt
2 teaspoons baking powder
dash nutmeg
oil for frying
butter and maple syrup for garnish

In a bowl whip together the eggs, milk, juice, honey, butter and oil until smooth. Fold in pineapple. Mix dry ingredients together, then fold in quickly. Do not overstir. Heat griddle, and lightly oil. Fry pancakes until golden, then flip. Cook until all batter is prepared. Serve with butter and syrup.

Serves 5-6 for breakfast.

Spicy Pear Muffins

1½ cups whole wheat flour
½ cup soy flour
1 tablespoon baking powder
½ teaspoon sea salt
1 teaspoon cinnamon
¼ teaspoon nutmeg
¼ teaspoon allspice
1 cup milk
1 egg, beaten
¼ cup butter, melted
¾ cup fresh pears, chopped

Sift together all the dry ingredients. Whip the milk, egg and butter together until smooth, then add in the pears. Add the dry ingredients into the pear mixture and stir only until all ingredients are wet. Fill oiled muffin tins ⅔ full and bake at 400 for 25 minutes. Remove and cool.

Makes 12 muffins.

Spicy Applesauce Cupcakes

½ cup butter
¾ cup honey
2 eggs
2 cups applesauce, unsweetened
2½ cups whole wheat pastry flour
1 teaspoon cinnamon
½ teaspoon mace
½ teaspoon cloves
2 teaspoons baking powder
½ teaspoon kelp powder
2 teaspoons vanilla
⅔ cup buttermilk
½ teaspoon lemon peel, grated
¾ cup walnuts, chopped finely
¼ cup currants

Cream butter and honey until fluffy. Stir in eggs and applesauce and whisk together. Combine all dry ingredients and set aside. Combine vanilla, buttermilk and lemon peel and whisk together. Alternately add in dry and wet ingredients to applesauce mixture. Fold in nuts and currants, then pour into lined muffin tins. Fill ½ full. Bake at 350 for 25-30 minutes. Remove and cool on wire rack.

Note: This can also be made into a cake. Fill an oiled, floured 13 X 9" pan and bake at 350 for 35-40 minutes. Test for doneness before removing by pressing lightly with finger. Cake will spring back slowly if done.

Makes 24.

Handy Hint: When thawing a frozen loaf of bread, add a paper towel in with the loaf to absorb the ice crystals.

Classic Struedel Dough

1⅓ cups unbleached flour
1 egg white
1 teaspoon safflower oil
1 teaspoon white vinegar
⅓ to ½ cup warm water
2½-3 cups filling (see index)

Sift flour and set aside. Whip the egg white until frothy, then add in oil and vinegar and whip until light. Add in the flour and about half the water and stir well. Continue adding in the water, a little at a time, until all the flour is absorbed. Knead the dough on a floured surface until it is smooth and elastic. Cover the dough with a towel and let rest 10 minutes. On a large floured surface, first roll the dough out to ⅛" thickness. Then continue to stretch the dough using the palms of both hands working together, one on each side of the dough. Every so often, stop and let the dough rest a minute. Continue until the dough is as thin as can be without tearing. Using half the filling, form a flat line on one third of the dough, then roll and repeat. Now roll the dough into its final rectangular shape, pinching any edges into the dough. Place on an oiled baking sheet and bake at 350 for 25 minutes. Struedel is done when filling bubbles in the middle and dough is browned. During the last five minutes of baking, brush with butter for perfect browning. Remove from oven and cool 10 minutes before slicing.

Filling note: Struedel is both a dessert and an entree, depending upon the filling you select. Successful fillings include fresh fruit fillings as well as savory vegetable, meat, curry or other crepe-like fillings. Avoid really creamy or drippy fillings, however, and keep with the more firm varieties. Either way, this is a glamorous dish.

Serves 6-8 desserts, or 4-5 entrees.

Authentic Boston Brown Bread

1 cup rye flour
1 cup cornmeal
1 cup graham flour or coarse whole wheat flour
⅔ teaspoon baking soda
1 teaspoon sea salt
⅔ cup blackstrap molasses
2 cups buttermilk
1 cup raisins

Combine all dry ingredients on waxed paper and set aside. Combine all wet ingredients in a bowl and mix well. Add in dry ingredients and stir until all is wet and sticky. Butter insides of 3 1-pound cans, and fill each ⅔ full of batter. Cover each can with foil, tightly. Set in simmering water ½ way up the cans. Cover the pot and steam bread 3 hours. Remove and cool 10 minutes, then shake from cans and serve with butter and honey.

Makes three loaves.

Banana Bran Muffins

½ cup warm milk
1 tablespoon yeast
¾ cup honey
½ cup safflower oil
2 medium bananas, mashed
1 cup bran
1⅞ cups whole wheat flour
½ teaspoon sea salt
1 teaspoon orange peel, grated

Combine milk and yeast and let stand 5 minutes. Meanwhile mix together the honey, oil, bananas and bran and let stand 5 minutes. Combine the two mixtures and stir well. Add in flour, salt and orange peel and stir well. Fill oiled and floured muffin tins ⅔ full, then set aside to let rise 12 minutes. Bake at 350 for 35 minutes, then remove and cool before serving.

Makes 12.

Festive Carrot-Zucchini Bread

2 cubes butter
1 cup honey
3 eggs
1 cup carrot, grated
1 cup zucchini, grated
1 teaspoon vanilla
2 cups whole wheat pastry flour
1 teaspoon baking soda
1 teaspoon sea salt
2 teaspoons cinnamon
¼ teaspoon nutmeg
¼ teaspoon baking powder
1 cup walnuts, chopped

Cream butter and honey until light and fluffy. Add in eggs and whisk until smooth. Fold in carrot and zucchini, then vanilla. Combine dry ingredients together, then stir into wet mixture until smooth. Fold in nuts, then pour into 2 oiled and floured 9X5" loaf pans. Bake at 325 for 1 hour or until bread tests done with toothpick. Remove and cool 10 minutes before removing from pans. Cool on wire racks.

Makes 2 loaves.

Handy Hint: If you think your baking powder is dead, add a teaspoonful to a cup of water. If it fizzes, it is still good.

Swedish Rye Bread

1½ tablespoons dry yeast
1 cup warm water
3 cups orange juice
½ cup honey
1 tablespoon blackstrap molasses
4 cups rye flour
1 cup do-pep (80% gluten flour)
5-6 cups whole wheat flour
1 tablespoon sea salt
1 tablespoon caraway seeds
1 tablespoon orange peel, grated

Dissolve yeast in water for 15 minutes, then add to a bowl containing the orange juice, honey, molasses, rye flour and do-pep. Whip with a wire whisk for 3 minutes. (This will develop the gluten more easily and quickly.) Add in 2 cups wheat flour, together with the remaining ingredients, stirring well. Continue adding whole wheat flour until dough is too stiff to stir. Turn dough onto a floured surface and knead dough until smooth and elastic. Dough is done when it stops accepting flour at a rapid rate. Place dough in an oiled bowl, cover and let rise until double. Punch dough down, shape into 3 loaves, or 6 cocktail rye loaves, place in oiled pans, cover and let rise until double. Bake at 350 for 50 minutes (loaves) or 25 minutes (cocktail loaves). Brush with oil when they come out of the oven, remove from pans and cool on their sides on a wire rack.

Makes 3 large or 6 smaller loaves.

Whole Wheat Brioche

Part of the romance of France is the Continental breakfast fare, including fresh brioche (bree OSH) warm from the oven. Now you can make them too, with full flavor and top of the morning nutrition.

1 cup milk
½ cup butter
1 teaspoon sea salt
¼ cup honey
1 tablespoon dry yeast
¼ cup warm water
4 eggs, beaten
1 teaspoon lemon peel, grated
dash nutmeg
4-5 cups whole wheat flour, very fine
butter to garnish

Scald milk, then add in butter, salt and honey. Set aside and cool. Dissolve yeast in warm water, then stir in eggs, lemon peel and nutmeg. Combine with cooled milk mixture. Add flour gradually to make a soft dough. Knead lightly on a floured surface until smooth and soft. Place dough in a large, buttered bowl, cover and let rise until double in bulk, about 1½ hours. Punch down and knead lightly again. Divide dough, one lump being ¾ dough and the other ¼ dough. Make 2½" balls with the larger dough lump, then make matching topknot balls with the smaller dough lump and press them lightly into the tops of the larger dough balls. Place in buttered muffin tins and brush with butter. Cover and let rise until double in bulk, then bake at 425° for about 12 minutes. Remove when lightly browned and cool on the wire racks. Serve warm or cool and freeze for later use.

Makes about 24.

Mellow Squash Bread

1 cup squash, cooked and sieved
2 tablespoons honey
1½ cups milk, scalded
1 teaspoon kelp powder
½ teaspoon pumpkin pie spice
1 teaspoon sea salt
1 tablespoon safflower oil
1 tablespoon dry yeast
½ cup warm water
5-7 cups whole wheat flour

Combine squash, honey, milk, kelp powder, spice and salt. Stir well, then add in oil. In a small cup combine the yeast and water until dissolved. Add into squash mixture, then begin adding in flour, one cup at a time, until dough is too thick to stir. Flour a flat surface and knead dough until smooth and elastic, adding flour to the board as long as the dough takes it readily. This will take only about 7-9 minutes. When dough is smooth, let rest, covered on the board for 15 minutes. Shape into 2 loaves and place in oiled baking pans. Cover and let rise in a warm place until double in bulk. Bake at 350 for 30-35 minutes, or until bread sounds hollow when thumped. Remove and cool slightly, then remove from pans and cool loaves on their sides on a wire rack. May wish to butter tops for more pliable crust.

Makes 2 loaves.

Handy Hint: Dough stuck on your counter. A credit card will scrape it up in no time.

One A Day Bran Muffins

1 cup bran
1 cup whole wheat flour
1 teaspoon baking powder
½ teaspoon kelp powder
½ teaspoon cinnamon
1 egg, beaten
1 cup buttermilk
¼ cup orange juice
¼ cup honey
2 tablespoons blackstrap molasses
½ cup dates, chopped
½ cup raisins, chopped
2 tablespoons butter, melted

Combine dry ingredients and toss well. Beat egg with buttermilk, juice, honey and molasses until smooth. Pour into dry ingredients and whip well. Fold in dates, raisins and butter and stir until incorporated. Oil muffin tins and fill to ⅔ full. Bake in a preheated 400° oven for 15 minutes, or until done.

Makes 12.

Sumptuous Breakfast Popovers

¾ cup whole wheat pastry flour
¼ cup corn flour
2 eggs
1 cup milk
2 tablespoons safflower oil

Preheat the oven to 450. Toss flours together. Whip eggs separately until light. Stir in flours and milk, then drizzle in oil. Whip well. Butter a muffin tin and set it in the oven until hot. Remove and fill muffin cups half full. Return to oven and bake at 450 for 20 minutes. Reduce heat to 350 and bake another 12-15 minutes. Remove and cool slightly, then serve.

Serving Suggestion: Fill each popover with 1 tablespoon cream cheese and 2 teaspoons strawberry jam. Garnish with maple syrup and sliced almonds. Serve immediately. There goes the diet.   Makes 12.

Golden Breakfast Granola

3 cups rolled oats
1 cup rolled wheat
1 cup wheat germ
¼ cup sesame seeds
½ cup sunflower seeds
¾ cup almonds, sliced
¼ cup milk powder
½ cup long chip coconut
½ cup safflower oil
¾ cup honey
2 teaspoons cinnamon
½ cup raisins

Combine first 8 ingredients in a large bowl and toss well. In a saucepan heat the oil and honey together. Mix in the cinnamon and boil 2 minutes. Pour over the dry ingredients and mix until all is wet. Spread onto a cookie sheet and bake at 350 for 10 minutes. Remove and stir completely. Add raisins in, mix again and return to the oven for 15 more minutes. Remove and cool. Store in a covered container.

Makes 9 cups cereal, or about 10 servings.

My Reliable Shortcake

2 cups whole wheat pastry flour
2 teaspoons baking powder
¼ teaspoon sea salt
¼ teaspoon kelp powder
¼ teaspoon baking soda
½ teaspoon lemon peel, grated
¼ cup butter
3 tablespoons lemon juice
9 tablespoons milk

Combine the dry ingredients together and toss well. Add in lemon peel and stir. Cut butter in with a pastry cutter or two knives until it disappears. Combine lemon juice and milk and let curdle 1 minute. Pour into batter and stir well. Drop from spoon onto oiled baking sheet, then flatten with a buttered hand. Bake at 400 for 12-14 minutes, or until golden.

Makes 12 average biscuits, or 6 "strawberry season" size.

New Old Country Croissants

1½ teaspoons yeast
¼ cup warm water
1 cup milk, room temperature
4 cups whole wheat flour
¼ teaspoon orange peel, grated
1 teaspoon sea salt
1½ cups butter

Dissolve yeast in water and set aside to dissolve. Add in milk and half the flour and stir well. Add in the rest of the flour, the orange peel and salt and stir well. Pour onto a floured surface and knead until smooth and elastic. Place in an oiled bowl and chill, covered for 30 minutes. Remove and roll out on a floured surface into a rectangle shape about ½" thick. Dot the center third of the rectangle with ¼ of the butter, then fold in one third of the dough over the butter, and dot it with ¼ of the butter as well. Cover that butter with the remaining one third of the dough, and roll out into another rectangle. Repeat this process once more, using up the butter. Roll into a rectangle when this is complete, then fold in and roll into a rectangle once more. Cover and chill 20 minutes. Remove and

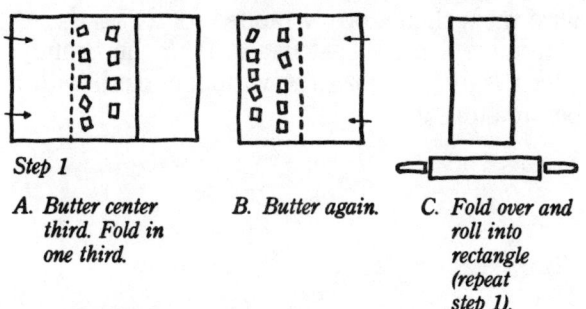

Step 1

A. Butter center third. Fold in one third.
B. Butter again.
C. Fold over and roll into rectangle (repeat step 1).

roll to ¼" thick and cut into 4" squares with a sharp knife. Cut each square diagonally and roll each triangle out slightly. Roll each triangle into a croissant, beginning with the longest side and rolling toward the point. Curve in the ends, and place on an oiled baking sheet. Cover and chill again for 15 minutes. Remove and bake at 400 for 10 minutes, then reduce to 350 for another 10-13 minutes. Remove and cool, then serve.

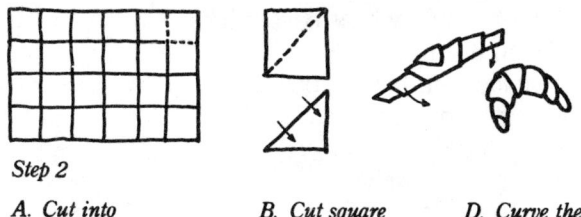

Step 2

A. Cut into 4-inch squares.
B. Cut square diagonally.
C. Roll triangle.
D. Curve the ends.

Note: The chilling is vital in this recipe which is why croissants are such a pain to make. But well worth it for the whole grain goodness and rich flavor they provide.

Makes about 3 dozen.

Buckwheat Maple Pancakes

1 cup buckwheat flour
1 cup whole wheat pastry flour
½ cup wheat germ
2 teaspoons baking powder
½ teaspoon kelp powder
pinch lemon peel, grated
2 eggs, beaten
1¾ cups buttermilk
¼ cup maple syrup
¼ cup butter, melted

Combine all dry ingredients and toss lightly. Beat lemon peel with eggs, buttermilk, syrup and butter until smooth. Pour wet ingredients into dry and whisk until smooth. Pour onto oiled, hot griddle and cook until golden, then turn once.

Variation: This recipe will also make a very easy buckwheat crepe. Thin this batter with up to ½ cup apple juice and follow instructions for crepe cooking. Makes very hearty dinner crepes. (See index)

Makes breakfast for 4.

Tartan Fruit Scones

2 cups whole wheat pastry flour
1½ cups oat flour
1 tablespoon baking powder
¼ cup honey
2 eggs, beaten
½ cup buttermilk
¼ cup safflower oil
½ cup raisins, chopped
2 teaspoons orange peel, grated
½ teaspoon ginger

Combine dry ingredients and toss well. Whip honey and eggs together until light, then add in buttermilk and oil. Pour wet ingredients into dry and stir until combined. Fold in raisins, orange peel and ginger and stir 30 seconds. Turn onto a floured surface and knead for 1 minute. Roll out to ½" thickness, then cut into 3" squares with a sharp, floured knife. Transfer to an oiled baking sheet with a spatula and bake at 425 for 8 minutes. Remove and serve immediately.

Variations: This classic scone is also excellent substituting the raisins for other dried fruits, or a festive mixture of citron and citrus peels. In any case, serve with lots of butter and berry jam.

Makes 24 scones.

Harvest Pumpkin Fruit Bread

½ cup butter
⅔ cup honey
1 egg, beaten
1 cup pumpkin puree
2 cups whole wheat pastry flour
½ teaspoon kelp powder
¼ teaspoon sea salt
2 teaspoons lemon rind, grated
2 teaspoons baking powder
¼ teaspoon cinnamon
¼ teaspoon nutmeg
dash cloves
dash mace
dash ginger
¼ cup raisins, chopped
½ cup combined chopped dates,
   figs or other dried fruit
¼ cup nuts, chopped
3 tablespoons Brandy (optional)

Cream butter and honey until fluffy. Whisk in egg and pumpkin puree. Toss dry ingredients together and add to wet. Fold in dried fruits and nuts and pour into a buttered loaf pan. Bake at 325 for 45-55 minutes, or until done. Cool on a wire rack, then store, wrapped for 24 hours before serving for best flavor. Pour the Brandy over the loaf, or soak the wrapping cloth with it before storing.

Makes 1 loaf.

Handy Hint: Keep all those leftover muffins, cornbread, bread heels and old garlic toast. When the freezer bag is full, make stuffing.

Holiday Date Nut Bread

⅔ cup dates, pitted and chopped
½ cup orange juice, very hot
¼ cup butter
½ cup honey
1 egg, beaten
1 tablespoon lemon rind, grated
1¾ cups whole wheat pastry flour
1 teaspoon baking powder
½ teaspoon kelp powder
¼ teaspoon nutmeg
1 teaspoon vanilla
⅔ cup pecans, chopped (or walnuts)

Combine the dates and juice and let stand until it comes to room temperature. Meanwhile, cream the butter and honey until fluffy, then whisk in the egg and lemon rind. Stir the dry ingredients together. Add the date mixture to the wet ingredients, then fold in the dry ingredients. Add in the vanilla and nuts and stir well. Pour into a buttered bread pan and bake at 350 for 45-50 minutes. Remove and cool slightly before removing from pan. Cool on a wire rack.

Makes 1 large date nut loaf.

Orange Sesame Waffles

2 cups whole wheat pastry flour
1 teaspoon baking powder
2 egg yolks
¼ cup sesame seeds
1 cup orange juice
⅓ cup milk
2 tablespoons milk powder
3 tablespoons safflower oil
2 egg whites, beaten

Combine flour and baking powder. Beat egg yolks until lemony, then stir in sesame seeds, orange juice, milk, milk powder and oil. Whisk in flour mixture until lumps are greatly reduced. Whip egg whites until stiff, and fold into waffle batter. Spoon onto heated, oiled waffle iron and bake until golden. Remove and serve immediately.

Serves 4.

Classic Banana Bread

¼ cup butter
⅓ cup honey
2 eggs, beaten
1 cup bananas, mashed
1⅞ cup whole wheat pastry flour
½ teaspoon kelp powder
2 teaspoons baking powder
1 tablespoon lemon rind, grated
⅔ cup walnuts, chopped
¼ teaspoon cinnamon

Cream the butter and honey together, then whisk in the eggs and bananas. Mix the dry ingredients together, then add to the wet, together with the lemon rind, walnuts and cinnamon. Stir well, then pour into a buttered bread pan. Bake at 325 for almost an hour, checking at 45 minutes. Remove and cool slightly before removing from pan, then continue cooling on a wire rack. Serve with butter.

Serving Suggestion: For a tempting spread that will turn this bread into a perfect dessert, cream ¼ cup cream cheese with ¼ cup butter and 2 tablespoons honey. Spread evenly and serve. Makes ⅔ cup. Store chilled.

Makes 1 large loaf.

Sweet Honey Wheat Berry Bread

1½ tablespoons dry yeast
4 cups warm water (100-110 degrees)
½ cup honey
10-11 cups whole wheat flour
1 tablespoon sea salt
1 cup carrot, shredded
1½ cups cracked wheat

Combine yeast, warm water and honey and let stand 15 minutes. Add in 4 cups flour, sea salt and carrot and stir well. Cover and let stand 15 minutes, then stir in 2 more cups flour and stir well. Add in cracked wheat, then add flour until dough is too stiff to stir. Pour onto a floured surface and knead flour in until dough is smooth and elastic and no longer absorbs flour at a rapid rate. Place in an oiled bowl, cover with a tea towel and set in a warm place to rise for about 1 hour or until double in bulk. Punch down, turn in bowl and let rise again for 20 minutes. Punch down, shape into 3 loaves and place into 3 oiled baking pans. Cover and let rise until double in bulk, then bake at 350 for 50 minutes, or until loaf sounds hollow when tapped. Remove and cool 5 minutes, then remove from pans and cool loaves on their sides on wire racks.

Note: for shiny loaves with tender crust, brush with butter when removed from the oven.

Makes 3 loaves.

Breakfast Corn Crepes

1 cup corn, drained
3 tablespoons cornstarch
¾ cups milk
2 tablespoons orange juice
⅓ cup whole wheat pastry flour
2 tablespoons butter, melted
pinch allspice
¼ teaspoon vanilla
1½ cups sour cream
2 teaspoons lemon peel, grated
¾ cup strawberry preserves

Combine corn, cornstarch, milk and orange juice in a blender and whirl until smooth. Add in flour, butter, allspice and vanilla and whirl again for 1 minute. Pour by tablespoons into oiled 6" crepe or frying pan. Turn pan to spread batter. When golden, flip and cook until lightly golden. When all crepes are cooked, fill with sour cream mixed with lemon peel, and strawberry preserves. Roll crepes, place in oiled baking dish and heat in the oven for 10 minutes at 300°. Remove and serve immediately.

Makes 16. Breakfast for 4.

Handy Hint: When making stuffing for a large crowd, mix it in a large plastic bag. No mess.

Quick-Stir
Orange Sesame Dinner Loaf

⅓ cup butter
⅓ cup honey
2 eggs, beaten
2 teaspoons orange rind, grated
1 cup orange juice
½ cup buttermilk (or plain yogurt)
3 cups whole wheat flour
1 teaspoon sea salt
1 tablespoon baking powder
½ cup sesame seeds, toasted
¼ cup walnuts, ground

Cream the butter and honey until fluffy, then whisk in the eggs, orange rind, juice and buttermilk. Toss dry ingredients and fold into wet mixture. Add in toasted seeds and nuts and stir well. Pour into oiled loaf pan and bake at 350 for 45-55 minutes. Remove and cool slightly, then remove from pan and continue cooling on a wire rack.

Note: This loaf gets easier to cut if allowed to stand, covered for 24 hours. Time also turns it into an excellent morning toast, responding well to ricotta cheese and marmalade spread upon it.

Makes 1 loaf.

Fresh Croutons

3 tablespoons olive oil
3 garlic cloves, bruised
3 tablespoons butter
6 slices whole grain bread, cubed

Heat the olive oil slowly in a 10" saute pan. Add in the garlic cloves and saute until the cloves brown completely. Stir frequently to guard against burning. Remove the garlic and add in the butter, stirring until the foaming subsides. Add in the cubed bread and toss lightly, sauteing about 8 minutes. Drain on paper towels briefly, then top your salad immediately. Store cooled croutons in a loosely-topped container.

Serving Suggestion: These croutons make not only a great salad garnish, but will serve well atop onion soup, casseroles and chowder.

Variation: Sprinkle 2 teaspoons minced parsley on top of draining croutons just prior to serving.

Makes about 3 cups.

Buffet Bread Sticks

2 cups whole wheat flour
½ cup sesame seeds
1 tablespoon honey
½ teaspoon sea salt
¼ teaspoon cinnamon
3 tablespoons safflower oil
¾ cup water
1 teaspoon orange peel, grated

Combine flour and sesame seeds and toss gently. In a blender combine the honey, salt, cinnamon, oil, water and orange peel and whip 30 seconds. Slowly add to dry ingredients until a stiff ball is formed. Knead on a floured surface for 2 minutes, then roll out and form 9" long dough pieces about ½" thick. Place them on an oiled baking sheet and bake at 350 for about 25-30 minutes, or until golden and crisping. Cool on wire racks and serve.

Makes 24.

Glorious Graham Crackers

1 cup rolled oats
½ cup bran
1½ cups whole wheat pastry flour
1 cup pitted dates, mashed
1 cup raisins, mashed
½ cup ground walnuts
¼ cup coconut, powdered
½ cup wheat germ
½ cup safflower oil
1¼ cups orange juice
¼ cup cashews
¼ lemon, seeded
1 tablespoon honey
2 tablespoons molasses
2 tablespoons melted butter

Toss together the oats, bran, flour, dates, raisins, walnuts, coconut and wheat germ. Cut the oil in with a pastry cutter. In a blender combine the orange juice, cashews, lemon, honey, molasses and butter. Pour this liquid into the oat combination and stir in until a stiff dough forms. Let stand 5 minutes, then knead briefly. Roll out on a floured surface to 3/8" thick. Cut into squares or other desired shapes, and bake on an unoiled baking sheet at 325 for 15-20 minutes, depending upon size. Cool on wire racks, then store in airtight containers.

Serving Suggestion: For a special breakfast treat, combine ½ cup cream cheese and ⅓ cup strawberry preserves. Spread on warm crackers from the oven.

Makes 3 pounds of crackers.

Scotch Oat Meal Crackers

The cracker without the added flavorings is the desired accompaniment to a delicate cheese or pâté. This classic oat cracker will delight the gourmet palate and satisfy the whole grain goodness balance I look for.

3 cups rolled oats
1 cup rolled rye
1 cup whole wheat flour
¾ cup unbleached flour
1 cup corn meal
¼ cup sesame tahini
½ cup soy flour
1 cup safflower oil
¾ cup honey
½ teaspoon soy sauce
1 teaspoon sea salt
½ teaspoon ground coriander
water
2 tablespoons sesame seeds

In a large bowl combine the five grains and flours and toss well. Add in the tahini, soy flour, oil, honey, soy sauce and seasonings. Mix well. Add in water gradually until a moist dough results which remains in a ball in the bowl. Pour onto a floured surface and gently knead to develop elasticity. Divide dough and roll out to 1/8" thickness. Place on oiled baking sheets and gently score into squares. Prick with a fork. Brush lightly with water and sprinkle with sesame seeds if desired. Bake at 300 for about 20 minutes, or until lightly golden.

Serving Suggestion: For holiday festivities, cut crackers out with interesting cookie cutter shapes for the season at hand. Your guests will love the change, not to mention the flavor!

Makes 2 pounds of crackers.

DESSERTS
Treats, Puddings, Ice Cream

Bourbon Balls

2½ cups Veranda Orange Cookies, crushed (see index)
or
vanilla wafer crumbs
½ cup honey
1 cup walnuts, chopped well
2 tablespoons carob powder, sifted
pinch cloves
1 teaspoon vanilla
¼ cup Bourbon
1 tablespoon milk powder
1 tablespoon cocoa powder

In a large bowl combine cookie crumbs, honey, walnuts, carob powder, cloves, vanilla and Bourbon. Mix well with wooden spoon, then mix with hands. Press into 1½" balls, and roll gently in powdered milk/cocoa powder mixture. Set aside, covered to age 1 day before eating.

Makes 2 dozen.

Fresh Pear Sherbet

2 lemons
⅓ cup honey
6 ripe summer pears (2 cups mashed)
3 tablespoons pear liqueur (optional)
2 egg whites

Grate the peel of one of the lemons. Juice both lemons and add peel to it in a large bowl. Add honey and whisk until smooth. Pare and chop pears, then add to the honey mixture. Add in liqueur, and stir after addition of each pear to keep them from turning brown. Add this whole mixture to a blender or food processor and puree. Whip egg whites until dry and fold the pear mixture into it. Pour into a crank-type ice cream freezer and freeze according to manufacturers directions. When firm, proof in freezer 3 hours before serving.

Makes about 1 quart.

Confetti Popcorn Balls

1 cup honey
¼ cup molasses
¾ cup raw sugar or date sugar (pulverized)
1 teaspoon vanilla
4½ quarts popped corn
dash sea salt
1 cup raw cashews, pieces
½ cup pecans, chopped
½ cup currants
¼ cup pumpkin seeds

Heat honey, molasses, raw sugar and vanilla over medium heat, stirring constantly, until the "hard ball stage" (a small amount dropped into cold water forms a firm but not brittle ball). In a large pot combine the popcorn and salt, then mix in the nuts, currants and seeds. Pour the hot syrup over all and toss to combine. Place 1 cup of mixture into a 12" square of waxed paper and form a ball. Place in a deep saucepan or stockpot. Repeat procedure until all balls are in the pot. Let cool completely, then remove and serve.

Makes 20.

Jungle Balls

1 cup brazil nuts
1 cup pecans
1¼ cups raisins
1¼ cups dates
3 tablespoons honey
1 tablespoon orange peel, grated
½ cup coconut, shredded

Combine brazil nuts and pecans in a food processor and chop until course. Add in raisins and dates and process again until about the size of dried peas. Add in honey and orange peel and mix until well blended. Form into 1" balls with your hands and roll in coconut. Set on waxed paper and chill 2 hours before serving. Store in covered container.

Makes 1½ pounds candy.

Luau Sharon's Hot Pineapple Rhumba

4 cups fresh cut pineapple chunks (conserve juice)
3 tablespoons whole wheat pastry flour
3 tablespoons butter
3 tablespoons honey
½ cup rum
½ cup fresh pineapple juice (add water to make enough if necessary)
½ gallon vanilla ice cream
¾ cup macadamia nuts, chopped
½ cup shredded coconut
¾ cup pitted dates, chopped

Cut pineapple into 1" chunks, and set aside. In low 13 X 9" pan combine flour, butter and honey with whisk. Whip in rum and juice, then add pineapple and stir to coat. Let stand 30 minutes, then stir again. Broil for 15 minutes, stirring occasionally to thicken. When thick and browning, serve over ice cream and garnish with macadamia nuts, coconut and dates.

Variations: This rhumba may also be made with nectarines or peaches. The rum may be substituted with Brandy or Sake.

Serves 10.

Raspberry-Currant Ice

3 cups fresh raspberries
1 cup rice currants
2 tablespoons honey
2 tablespoons lemon juice

Combine all ingredients in a bowl and mash well. Pour into a blender and whirl 30 seconds, until smooth. Pour into a freezer tray and freeze 4 hours. Remove and serve in long-stem glasses.

Serves 6.

Serving Suggestion: This ice is perfect for dessert to a heavy meal, and possibly as a palate cleanser to a first course. It may also be transformed into an evening cocktail. Simply combine frozen ice with 1½ ounces rum in a blender and serve "slushy" style. Makes 8 cocktails.

Indecent-Kabobs

This shameless combination of decadent ingredients will delight your guests and put pressure on your liqueur collection. Never fear, however, for the broiling removes the alcohol.

8 chunks watermelon (1 X 1½" seeded)
¼ cup ruby Port
8 slices dried apricot
1 tablespoon Kirsch
1 tablespoon orange juice
2 large nectarines, pitted and sliced into 16 wedges
1 large banana, sliced into 8 pieces
¼ cup butter, melted
⅓ cup graham cracker crumbs
3 ounces cream cheese
5 tablespoons orange juice
1½ tablespoons Triple Sec
2 teaspoons orange peel, grated
¼ cup walnuts, chopped finely

Combine watermelon and Port and soak 1 hour. Combine apricots, Kirsch and orange juice and soak 1 hour. Thread watermelon, apricots, nectarine slices and banana chunks onto skewers. Roll in melted butter, then roll in graham cracker crumbs. Place under broiler for 6-8 minutes, turning once. In the meantime, combine cream cheese, orange juice and Triple Sec in a small saucepan and heat slowly. Whisk until smooth and steaming, then add orange peel and heat 1 minute more. Cover and set aside. When skewers come out of broiler, top with sauce, garnish with walnuts and serve immediately.

Serves 4.

Strawberries Sabayon Monique

This classic sabayon sauce is perfect for many things, including the garnishing of perfect spring fruits.

1 dry quart fresh strawberries, cleaned and capped
2 egg yolks
2 tablespoons honey
1 tablespoon water
1 tablespoon heavy cream
1 teaspoon Brandy

Assemble strawberries among 6 serving dishes. In a small saucepan whisk together the egg yolks, honey and water. Turn on the heat and whisk over low flame until thickened. Add in cream and Brandy and continue whisking until thick and smooth. Pour over fresh fruits and place under broiler 1 minute for a touch of golden brown. Serve immediately.

Serving variation: Sabayon sauce has many uses. It is perfect served over ice cream, puddings and other fresh fruits. Broiled warm or chilled, it is marvelously rich and satisfying.

Serve 6. Makes ½ cup.

Fast Mango Flip

1½ cups mango pulp, mashed
½ cup orange juice
2 tablespoons Grand Marnier
1 cup whipping cream
½ cup macadamia nuts, chopped

In a blender combine the mango pulp, juice and liqueur until smooth. Pour into a bowl. In another bowl whip the cream until very firm. Fold cream into mango mixture, then spoon into serving dishes. Chill up to 4 hours before serving. Garnish with nuts at serving time.

Makes 8 servings.

Rainbow Frozen Yogurt

1 cup blueberries
1 cup strawberries, mashed
½ cup pineapple, crushed
½ cup papaya, mashed
1 banana, mashed
1 cup honey
½ cup shredded coconut, unsweetened
¼ cup lemon juice
1 tablespoon lemon peel, grated
1 tablespoon vanilla
1 teaspoon nutmeg
3 eggs, separated
¼ teaspoon sea salt
2 quarts plain yogurt

Combine fruits, honey, coconut, lemon juice and peel into a large saucepan and bring to a boil. Simmer, stirring constantly for 4 minutes. Remove from heat and add vanilla and nutmeg. Stir and cool. Beat egg yolks until lemony. Stir a few tablespoons fruit mixture into egg yolks, then add yolk mixture back into fruits and stir. Beat egg whites and sea salt until stiff. Add plain yogurt into fruit mixture until smooth. Fold egg whites in only until disbursed. Transfer mixture into a 1 gallon ice cream freezer and process following manufacturer's direction. Use 4 parts ice to 1 part rock salt. When mixture is firm, remove dasher and proof in deep freeze for up to 4 hours before serving (if you can wait that long).

Makes 1 gallon.

Handy Hint: Line cake pans with kitchen parchment rather than waxed paper. It is more heat resistant and lacks wax.

Charlotte's Carob Pudding

2 cups tofu
1 cup cream cheese
½ cup butter, melted
½ cup honey
1 banana
¼ cup lemon juice
1 teaspoon lemon rind, grated
2 tablespoons carob powder
2 teaspoons vanilla
¼ teaspoon cloves

Drain and press tofu to remove excess water. In blender or food processor combine the tofu, cream cheese, butter and honey. When whipped until creamy pour into a bowl and set aside. Without cleaning blender, add in banana, lemon juice and all other ingredients. Puree these ingredients until completely smooth. Add back as much of the tofu mixture as your appliance will hold and mix 1 minute. Pour into bowl containing remaining tofu mixture and beat with a wire whisk until smooth and completely combined. Pour into a serving dish or individual dishes and chill 4 hours.

Serves 6.

Chocolate Rum Sauce

This fast and easy sauce can be the fancy part of an easy ice cream dessert.

6 ounces semi-sweet chocolate
⅓ cup water
2 tablespoons butter
¼ cup whipping cream
2 tablespoons rum

In the top of a double boiler, over hot water, combine the chocolate and water and stir until melted. Stir in the butter and cream and whisk until smooth, then add the rum and whisk again. Do not allow this mixture to boil. Serve immediately over ice cream or dessert crepes.

Makes 1 cup sauce. Tops 4-6 desserts generously.

Sweet Plum Sorbet

8 ripe plums, pitted
  (Santa Rosa or purple suggested)
¾ cup water
1 cup orange juice
½ cup honey
¼ cup Kirsch (optional)
  or
¼ cup cherry juice
2 tablespoons lemon juice
1 tablespoon orange peel, grated
⅛ teaspoon cinnamon

Chop plums, then combine with water, orange juice and honey in a saucepan. Bring to a boil, then simmer 12 minutes. Remove and cool slightly, then puree in a blender or food processor. Pour into a bowl, and add in Kirsch, lemon juice, orange peel and cinnamon. Whisk in until well blended. Set aside to cool at room temperature, then place in ice cube trays and freeze (may freeze in mechanical freezer also, to manufacturer's instructions). When almost firm, remove and whip. Return to freezer for final freezing. Serve as a light dessert.

Makes 1 quart.

Dante's Heavenly Bananas

2 large oranges
⅓ cup honey
¾ stick butter
5 tablespoons rum
1 lemon
6 ripe bananas, peeled
1 quart vanilla ice cream
1 dry quart strawberries, cleaned and capped

Grate the peel of one orange. Heat honey and butter and add in peel. Saute lightly. Juice the oranges and add to butter mixture. Add in rum. Juice the lemon and add in that juice. Heat until bubbling softly, then add in whole bananas. Baste lightly 2 minutes per side. If sauce is not thick, remove bananas and rapid-boil sauce until syrupy. Return bananas to pan and baste once, turning off heat. Scoop ice cream into 6 serving dishes, top with strawberries and then top all with one banana each and sauce to garnish. Serve immediately.

Serves 6.

Coeur a la Creme

This is traditionally a very rich and upper crust dessert. It has a very special taste and delights all the senses.

2 pounds cream cheese
1 pint heavy cream
4 egg whites
sea salt

Sieve the cream cheese, then beat the cream into it until smooth. Beat the egg whites until dry and fold into the cheese mixture. Add in a pinch of sea salt and mix well. Drain overnight through meshing, cheesecloth or traditional coeur a la creme heart-shaped cups. Serve surrounded by fresh berries of your choice.

Serves 8-10 generously.

Barb's Mountain

One evening in the late spring, after a particularly tiring massage therapy class, our instructor Barb appeared with a reward for her diligent students. It rivals the banana split in taste and decadence.

1 dry quart raspberries
1 dry quart strawberries
2 ripe bananas
4 shortcake biscuits (see index)
½ pint whipping cream
1 tablespoon honey
1 teaspoon vanilla
1 pint vanilla ice cream

Combine berries in a large bowl. Slice bananas into them, toss and set aside. Slice biscuits and place half in each large serving bowl. Whip cream with honey and vanilla until firm. Place 1 scoop ice cream on each biscuit half. Top with berries. Top berries with other biscuit half, then more ice cream, berries and finally whipped cream. Crown each dessert with an available strawberry and serve. And, as they say at my house, "Totally Awesome."

Serves 4.

Pineapple-Coconut Pudding

2½ cups milk
2 cups coconut, grated
½ cup long grain brown rice
¾ cup pineapple, chopped and drained
½ teaspoon sea salt
¼ cup honey
¼ teaspoon cinnamon
⅛ teaspoon ginger
¼ cup raisins

Scald milk. Add in coconut and cook 10 minutes, being careful not to boil. Add all remaining ingredients into the pan and place over a double boiler. Cook, covered, for 1 hour, stirring occasionally. Let stand 10 minutes before serving.

Serves 8.

Honey Mousse

This light and versatile dessert is perfect for any meal and fits the rigors of a tight schedule. Make it ahead, even the day before.

5 eggs, separated
1 cup honey
1 teaspoon vanilla
pinch cream of tartar
1½ cups blueberries
2 teaspoons arrowroot
¼ cup honey

Cream egg yolks, honey and vanilla in a heavy cooking pot. Whip with an electric mixer until smooth, then turn on the heat underneath. Continue to whip over the heat until it boils, then reduce to simmering. Continue whipping until mixture doubles in volume. Transfer to a glass bowl and allow to cool completely. Whip egg whites together with the cream of tartar until stiff. Gently fold into the cooled honey mixture. Chill in bowl, mold or individual serving dishes for 4 hours. Meanwhile, combine berries, arrowroot and honey over heat and cook until thickened, about 10 minutes. Stir constantly, allowing mixture to come to a boil, then immediately reducing heat to simmer. Cool completely, then serve with honey mousse.

Mousse serves 8.

Handy Hint: Pack an iced cake in a lunchbox without disturbing the frosting. Simply cut the cake in half horizontally and make a sandwich with the cake, the frosting in the middle.

Grandma's Brown Rice Pudding

1 cup brown rice
2 cups water
2 cups milk
½ teaspoon sea salt
½ cup raisins
2 eggs, beaten
3 tablespoons honey
1 teaspoon vanilla
½ teaspoon cinnamon
dash nutmeg

Combine rice and water and simmer 40 minutes, or until rice is tender. Add in milk, salt, raisins, eggs, honey, vanilla and cinnamon and stir well. Pour into a buttered 8 cup baking dish, cover and bake at 350 for 20 minutes. Uncover and garnish with nutmeg and continue baking uncovered for 5-8 minutes, or until set. Remove and cool slightly, then serve.

Serves 6-8.

Creamy Buttermilk Mousse

2 envelopes unflavored gelatin
1 cup buttermilk
1 cup orange juice
1 cup whipping cream
1½ cups cantaloupe balls, small
12 strawberries
1 cup nectarines
½ cup blueberries
½ cup walnuts, chopped

Sprinkle gelatin over buttermilk in a saucepan and let stand 5 minutes to soften. Heat buttermilk just to the boiling point and allow to simmer 3 minutes. Add in orange juice and set aside to cool. Chill until consistency of egg whites, then remove from refrigerator. Whip cream until firm and fold into buttermilk gel. Gently fold in fruits and nuts and pour into a lightly buttered 10 cup mold. Chill 4 hours or overnight. Unmold and serve surrounded with fresh fruit.

Serves 10.

Cherries Jubilee

One of the romantic desserts to serve, this recipe makes it fast and easy for everyone.

2 pounds Bing cherries, pitted (fresh or canned)
2 tablespoons orange peel, grated
½ cup orange juice
2 tablespoons red currant jelly
1 teaspoon cinnamon
1 tablespoon cornstarch
½ cup cherry juice
¼ cup orange juice
¼ cup Brandy
1 quart vanilla ice cream

Combine the cherries, peel, juice, jam and cinnamon in a heavy saucepan and heat until boiling. Reduce heat to simmer, cover and cook 10 minutes. Combine cornstarch with cherry and orange juices, then add to cherries. Stir until thick, stirring frequently. Heat Brandy in a separate saucepan, then light and pour over cherries mixture. Spoon flaming cherries over ice cream and serve immediately.

Serving Suggestion: Do the last step at the table in front of your guests so they can enjoy the excitement of the dessert and also learn how it is done!

Serves 6.

Rhubarb Crisp

½ cup butter
½ cup whole wheat pastry flour
4 cups granola (see index)
1 teaspoon cinnamon
1 tablespoon lemon juice
3 cups rhubarb sauce*
½ cup sour cream

Cut butter and flour together until mixed. Add in granola and toss until combined. Include cinnamon and lemon juice and stir until well mixed. Pour half this mixture into a buttered 8" baking dish, then press. Pour rhubarb sauce on top, spreading evenly. Top with remaining granola mixture and press firmly. Bake at 350 for 25 minutes, then cool slightly and serve with a dollop of sour cream.

Serves 8.

*Homemade rhubarb sauce is easily made. Wash and trim stalks, cutting into 1" pieces. For every pound of rhubarb used, cook with ½ cup honey and ¼ cup water. Cover and steam over lowest heat, stirring occasionally until thick and tender. Cool and use.

Makes about 3 cups per pound.

Shimmering Jewels

1 envelope unflavored gelatin
⅓ cup honey
⅓ cup fresh orange juice
1½ cups Champagne
1 tablespoon creme de cassis

Combine gelatin, honey and orange juice in saucepan and let stand 5 minutes. Add heat and stir until steaming. Add in Champagne and continue to heat. Stir gently to avoid foaming, and bring to the boiling point. Remove and cool slightly, then add liqueur. Pour into 8 X 8" pan and chill 4-6 hours. Just before serving, cut into ¾" squares and serve in Champagne glasses.

Serves 4.

HERBS
Terminology, Herbs, Recipes

Herbs

The world of herbs and spices, of flavorful leaves, pods and twigs is one familiar and foreign at the same time. While most of us would not think twice about sprinkling pepper on our food, we sometimes hesitate to mix cayenne in water and drink it for improved circulation to the hands and feet. Yet these two seeds, members of the same family, are kept apart in our minds by separate points of reference.

As recent as one or two generations ago, common herbal remedies were a familiar part of home health care. One could count on a strong liniment, a peculiar cough liquid, a strong tea or a combination of ground herbs held together with a biscuit for smooth sailing down the gullet to obtain the required relief from life's little discomforts. Even daily sipping of light teas or spring tonics was considered a sure shield from the long-term effects of a hard but hardy lifestyle.

The manufacture of household commodities from scented soaps to soothing creams and potions, not to mention leafy combinations for winter clothing storage and even compounds to keep housebound pets free of parasites relied upon the cultivation and proper understanding of certain vital ingredients. Logically, because of the need for these items, they were grown in the family garden, right along with the vegetables and fruits. Happily, as vegetables ripened at the same time herbs matured and stock was slaughtered, culinary use of these plants was also incorporated into family life. Many herbs are even eaten "straight", as it were, for their delightful flavor as well as their healthful advantages.

The following list of herbs and spices will include some you may eat every day as well as some you may have wanted to try but may not have known quite how to do it. Still others, which you may enjoy now will offer exciting alternatives for further exploration. Recipes for potpourri, bouquet garni, tea mixtures, poultices, perfume, bathing combinations, facial packs and other delights follow the explanations. In any instances of personal sensitivity to any combination offered, please refrain from further use. Your body will be telling you about a private allergy you may not be aware of. And although sensitivity to these more common herbals is not widespread, it is always best to listen to your body above the advice of a general rule.

A few terms you may discover in your new trek into herbals are pharmacological in nature, and easy to understand. All "baffling with terminology" attempts are lost on me. I just look them up! Here are a few to help you.

Decoction: A tea made of roots and bark of a plant. To make a proper decoction, combine 1 tablespoon of cut root or bark, or 1 tablespoon powdered herb and boil gently for 30 minutes, covered. Let stand 10 minues, then strain.

Fomentation: A clean cloth soaked, then wrung out in a hot infusion or decoction and applied to an affected area. This is considered a lighter treatment than a poultice, and generally less effective in the long run.

Infusion: A tea made of the leaves and blossoms of a plant. To make a proper infusion, use 1 teaspoon of powdered leaf or blossom (or 1 tablespoon loose herb) in one cup boiling water. Immediately remove from heat, stir and cover for 10 minutes. Strain and use.

Extraction: Herbal oil is made through extraction. Place the powdered herb in the top of a double boiler, then cover with enough olive oil to wet the herb well. Cook over simmering water, uncovered for 3 hours. Allow the mixture to cool and settle, then strain into a dark vial for later use.

Poultice: A wet, warm herbal pack applied locally to the body. Follow the specific poultice recipe, making sure to use fresh herbs which you crush or bruise just prior to preparation. If no specific liquid is mentioned, mineral water is appropriate. Always use a clean cloth for application, spreading the ingredients evenly. Leave poultice on affected area for several hours for maximum results. A poultice works by drawing toxins out and also by creating extra circulation or heat in an affected area. Never re-use a poultice.

Tincture: An herbal suspension in vinegar or alcohol. Combine about 4 ounces of herbs in 1 pint of vinegar (apple cider) or alcohol (100 proof vodka will do) and cover. Shake daily for 2 weeks, then strain and use.

Elixir: A sweet, alcoholic medicinal liquid. Combine 1 ounce appropriate herbs to 1 cup water and boil together in a glass saucepan with lid for 10 minutes. Remove from heat, add honey to taste and cool. Strain, then add ¾ cup 100 proof vodka. Store in a dark bottle 2 days then use as needed. Adults, a teaspoon every hour or so. Children, a teaspoon every 3-4 hours.

In addition, these may clear up a few questions as well:

Anodyne: a pain killer.

Astringent: used to close the pores, and to clear facial skin.

Castile: generally meaning the use of olive oil in soap as opposed to tallow or other animal products.

Demulcent: soothes the mucus surfaces internally and protects internal inflammations.

Diaphoretic: makes you perspire.

Diuretic: creates free flow and increased volume in the kidneys and excretory system. Causes increased urination.

Essense: One ounce essential oil dissolved in 1 cup rubbing alcohol.

Essential Oil: A steam distillation of the fragrance center of the herb.

Extract: a concentrate made by combining the herb with a solvent.

Nervine: a substance which soothes the nerves.

Restorative: brings back normal vigor.

Spirit: a 10% alcohol distillation of an herb.

Unguent: an oily combination which liquifies when applied to the body.

Water Bath: gently heating delicate ingredients. A double boiler will accomplish this.

When purchasing herbs, be aware that they come in several forms. Select the form which best applies to your application of it.

Powdered: when an herb has been pulverized.

Ground: when a coarse powder is made.

Cut and Sifted: chopped herb from which twigs and powder are removed.

Pieces: large pieces of root or bark or twig.

Whole: usually meant for seeds, pods and flowers. Left whole for maximum potency at the time of use, when they are generally crushed.

Fresh: generally meant for culinary herbs, to be brought crisp and unbruised from the produce section, or plucked from the garden likewise.

Herbs

Alfalfa: used as a tea from the leaves, a decoction from the seeds and a sprout from the seeds. A healthful, general restorative herb, giving vitamins, minerals and protein.

Aloe *(also aloe vera)*: juice of the aloe leaves is used internally to soothe and regulate the digestive system. Externally it is excellent for wounds, burns, insect bites and all sorts of skin ailments. Many kitchens have a plant growing on the sill for instant first aid.

Basil *(also sweet basil)*: important culinary herb, found in Italian cooking, tomato-based soups and stews, jambalaya, salads, dressings and egg dishes. Brewed as a tea and also used as a poultice to draw out insect bites. Easily grown in temperate climate.

Benzoin gum: a balsam resin used as a base for many herbal combinations to fix the fragrance in a sachet and to make the aromatic effect in perfumes more long-lasting and pungent. Available in pharmacies.

Camomile *(also chamomile)*: one of the oldest-known herbs, this mild and pleasant flower calms the body and the soul. Excellent for the skin when applied as a cool tea, and perfect as a nervine when taken internally. It will also calm the stomach. Grown in gardens easily, it is also a companion plant to your garden, as it wards off unwanted pests.

Cayenne *(also capsicum anum)*: very hot pepper, suitable for eating with most fish, fowl and beast. Excellent in hot sauces and a perfect accent to a souffle, omelet or custard dish. As an herb, recommended to improve circulation externally by sprinkling some in the shoes. Internally, this pepper will improve circulation and tend to help in warding off cold symptoms.

Chive: a member of the onion family, accenting meats and cream soups. Giving a touch of onion flavor to egg, cream and cheese dishes. Good for general health and for stimulating the appetite. An excellent window sill herb.

Comfrey: the queen of herbs, offering tasty tea, healing qualities in the allantoin it contains for internal and external aid, and the most hardy herb known. A spring tonic of fresh leaves is excellent, as are steamed fresh leaves as a spring vegetable. Use as a base for a poultice or healing mixture. With room for only one herb in the garden, this would be my choice. I would contain it, however, as it is a classic over-achiever.

Coriander *(also cilantro and Chinese parsley)*: an Old World herb, carrying legend and tradition with it through many nations. Found in soups, broths, sausage, curries, pickling and guacamole, green sauce and pesto it offers a spicy aroma. Used to flavor gin. An effective carminitive for the stomach.

Dandelion: the tender green leaves are excellent in salad, wilted salad and steamed as an early spring vegetable. High in vitamin A, it is excellent for the cleansing of the system after a winter of dull foods. Used as a tea, it is an effective diuretic. The roasted roots are found in non-caffienated coffee substitutes.

Dill: a tall, rangy member of the herb garden, it offers its oils whenever you brush up against it. Very aromatic, the seeds and foliage are used. Found in hearty soups, with lamb, in pickling especially cucumbers and sauerkraut, in delicate sauces to accent egg or shrimp dishes and in salads and breads, often accented by cheese. Helpful in relieving stomach gas and colic. Soothes. For hiccups, boil in vinegar or white wine and breathe the steam.

Fennel: this licorice-flavored seed is widely used in soups, with mussels, sausage, in stewed fruits, salad dressings and sauces and in flavorful liqueurs and desserts. It is useful in scenting soaps and perfumes and is used as an antidote to poisonous foods. It also stimulates the body, and is used not only for nursing mothers but as a safe and effective diuretic.

Garlic: not an official herb, but used in that capacity in stews, with all meats, in butter and dressings. A famous bulb, its uses in restoring and maintaining health are numerous. Most useful in curing the common cold and found in liquid form in combination with parsley, it will aid all symptoms. Also handy hung in the doorway of your home to ward off vampires (it's worked at my house so far). I increase garlic consumption at my house during the winter and it appears to keep colds and flu away from our door as well. (Handy garlic hint: Instead of peeling a garlic clove, which is boring and messy, simply gently mash it once under the tap of a broad side of a knife. Once "bruised" in this manner, the garlic skin comes off immediately.)

Ginseng: the herb of ancient China, this root is known for its effect on long life and sustained energy. Taking at least 6 years to mature, the root resembles the human form. Grown in many temperate zones, it may be found in the U.S. as well as China and Korea, where it is grown and regulated by the government.

Golden Seal: an effective, non-irritating healer of the surfaces of the body both externally and internally. Its antiseptic and soothing qualities are well known. It is used as a tea, wash, poultice and fabric dye for fine silks and cottons. Restores the body.

Henna: an herb used as a dye and cosmetic since Egyptian times. Used to color or highlight the hair, it is also used to color fingernails, skin, chest and stomach. Perfume may also be made of its flowers. A decoction of the leaves is used against headache. Henna has experienced a return to popularity recently. Always separate a permanent and a henna treatment by 8 weeks.

Jojoba: oily seed of a plant grown in warmer climates. The oil aids against baldness, dandruff, hair loss, psoriasis and seborrhea. Though wild claims have been made for it in recent press, it is effective in some kinds of restorative hair treatment, especially when combined with scalp massage, stress-management vitamin program and cleansing diet. Happily, this new cash crop will encourage the use of jojoba oil rather than whale oil in cosmetic manufacture.

Kelp: an herb from the sea; any of the brown sea kelps. Its most common use is in the powdered form as a salt substitute. It contains 1/16th the sodium of table salt, and resembles the salt taste accurately. It may be substituted for salt in all except yeast-rising bread recipes, where it may be used for about half the salt required. (Don't try that in this book, as the salt has already been adjusted.) Kelp is beneficial in balancing the adrenal system, the pituitary and thyroid. In other words, kelp assists the body regulators to do the best possible job of maintaining optimal metabolic balance. Kelp figures into many dieting systems, especially the kelp-B^6-vinegar-lecithin diet combination because the system is encouraged to maintain homeostasis. People with "sleepybear" syndrome in the morning will wake up easier, while others will have more control over reproductive problems, leg cramps and even diabetes. Kelp is even found in facial cleansers, as it is beneficial to the skin when applied topically. It is available in powdered and tablet form.

Lavendar: in the garden, it is a sure attraction for bees and will insure pollination due to its high fragrance. Used since medieval times to scent rooms, acts as a base ingredient to sachets and sleeping pillows and as an oil in perfumes, soaps and cosmetics, lavendar is also used as a douche, a mild cologne and a splash for acne, facial puffiness and insect repellant. A mild tea will settle the stomach, and a facial sauna will relieve a headache.

Licorice root: another herb of antiquity, this sweet root is used to flavor sweet desserts, liqueur and candy. A decoction will relieve thirst, aid peptic ulcer, relieve mucus buildup and act as a laxative in a mild way. Its soothing action on the throat makes it a popular ingredient for lozenges and gargles.

Marjoram: a general culinary enhancement, found in cream fish soups, most meats, with many vegetables, eggs, sauces and in bouquet garni. It complements oregano and may accompany it most places. Made as a foot soak it will relieve the body of a heavy feeling. It helps in removing bruises from the skin and will aid the joints when stiff.

Oregano: culinary uses widely associated with Italian cooking. Excellent with pasta sauces, seafoods, zucchini and eggplant dishes, it is also tasty in oil/vinegar salad dressings. Especially good as a fresh herb in green salad.

Papaya: the leaves and fruit of this herb are valuable. The leaves are used as a digestive aid: as a tea, and are combined with other herbs as a general tonic and calmative. The fruit, when unripe, is an excellent food steamed and served to a nursing mother. Ripened, the fruit contains papain, a strong digestive enzyme used to aid digestion, and also found in commercial meat tenderizer. A tablespoon of papaya fruit in ¾ cup meat marinade will do the trick.

Parsley: the common table herb, often left behind as a garnish of only visual value. Loaded with vitamin A, C and chlorophyll, it is of great value to the body. Eaten at the end of a meal, it clears the palate and freshens the breath, including heavy garlic. Most commercial breath candies use parsley to obtain their chlorophyll. So save your money at the candy counter and eat what has been on your plate all this time! My favorite exotic way to eat parsley is deep-fried in tempura batter. Crunchy and exquisite. Parsley is beneficial to the body as a cleanser, and will keep the stomach in top condition.

Peppermint: probably the most common herb associated with tea drinking. This tingling, stimulating herb is used in numerous personal hygiene products from toothpaste to shampoo and has an antibacterial effect. It is used to flavor candy, ice cream and soft drinks as well as a widely used aid to gas, nausea and upset stomach. It is a pleasing, refreshing herb which grows easily in poor soil with little care. There are numerous mints to choose from, and they are interesting to cultivate.

Raspberry leaf: used in Europe for centuries as an aid to female problems of all sorts from easier menstruation to easier labor and increased milk supply. Additionally, the tea aids the body's infection-fighting ability and can fight sore throat, gland swelling and body ache. The cooled tea is also helpful externally as a skin wash for wounds. A touch of peppermint and a slice of lemon makes this tea more flavorful, especially if it is drunk daily throughout a pregnancy.

Rosehip: the seedpod of the rose, most commonly gathered from wild roses growing in clearcut areas and along railroad tracks. Picked in the late summer when they are ripe as peaches. Cut, seeded, mashed and dried, they are powdered. Very high in vitamin C, this powder is included in mixtures and infusions to relieve colds, fever, kidney problems, bruises and circulatory sluggishness. Tart, it also makes an excellent jelly similarly delicate to quince jelly.

Rosemary: very pungent member of the evergreen and mint families. Found throughout culinary endeavor at the meat and potatoes end of the menu. Used in incense and perfumes, lotions and aromatics, rosemary is credited with relieving headache, rheumatic pain, prostate problems. It stimulates the appetite, combats baldness and lifts the spirits. Moths are discouraged from living in its presence. Oil of rosemary will treat hair to a regenerative treatment, leaving it shiny and vibrant. A restorative.

Saffron: dried stigmas of the saffron crocus, 75,000 needed for one ounce. Found in special recipes such as bouillabaisse, paella, chicken dishes and rice combinations, it has a very distinctive flavor and color. Used by royalty for dyeing cloth (hence: royal saffron) it has adopted the air of exclusive use for certain dishes. And though it is expensive, it is easily grown and harvested.

Sage: pungent herb, used most commonly in stuffing with fowl, and beast. Used sparingly outside of meat dishes. Medically, sage is valuable in breaking up mucus and chest congestion. This can be accomplished with tea, or by smoking or breathing fumes. The decoction is also an aid to soothing skin, sore feet and to calm the nerves.

Tarragon: a prolific fresh herb with a slight anise flavor, tarragon is best used fresh. Found in fish, salads, with veal, chicken and other fowl, cream sauces and salad vinegars it is used generally by adding large amounts for savory effect. As a tea it will sweeten the breath and relax one enough for easy sleep.

Thyme: another member of the mint family, thyme has an aromatic and biting flavor. Found in chowders, fish dishes, roasts, fowl, and with certain vegetable combinations including tomatoes, onions, zucchini and eggplant. The flowers of this herb make a remarkable honey. Easy on the skin, the infusion is used as an antiseptic, carminitive and tonic. Oil of thyme is enlisted for its stimulating, disinfecting and deodorant properties. Found in cough drops, hair tonics and ointments, thyme also treats genital problems from external swellings to internal flushings.

Vanilla: a member of the orchid family, and needing special bees for pollination. The vanilla bean pod is used in perfume, potpourri and for flavoring foods. It is also used as a stimulant, an antihysteric and an aphrodisiac.

Fines Herbes

This delicate herbal combination of tarragon, parsley, chives and chervil is added during the last seconds of preparation into soups, sauces and entree egg or cheese dishes. By fine mincing just prior to addition, these herbs release and combine their sensitive oils and impart a crowning touch to the foods they season. Only fresh herbs will do for this effect. Though some other gentle herbs may be used, this is the traditional combination.

1 teaspoon tarragon
1 teaspoon parsley
1 teaspoon chives
1 teaspoon chervil

Clean and pat dry all herbs. Mince together with a very sharp knife. Sprinkle over an omelet, cheese souffle, cream soup or Hollandaise sauce. Makes 1 heaping tablespoon garnish. Garnish a dish for 6-8.

Aloe Sunburn Poultice

Aloe vera works because it is cool, it heals and it is very similar to the body's own skin make-up. It is perfect alone, or in this case, in combination with other herbs to promote fast healing of the skin.

½ cup aloe vera gel (not juice)
3 large comfrey leaves, fresh
1 tablespoon wheat germ oil

In a small blender container, combine the ingredients and blend until they are pureed. Spread over the affected area as often as needed for relief from sunburn.

Bouquet Garni

This bundle of herbs, tied either in cheesecloth or simply wadded inside a celery stock or onion half, is used to flavor a stock. It is meant to be discarded after one use and generally enhances the stock, sauce or end product. Traditionally, fresh herbs are used and they usually include parsley, bay leaf, thyme and chervil. Occasionally celery, leeks, clove, marjoram and chives are included. Use whole or sprig whenever possible, avoiding powdered or overly crumbled herbs. Use bouquet garni during the last half hour of a cooking sequence, then discard. You may wish to make several bundles at a time and store them together in an airtight container for handy use. The following recipe makes 24 small bundles, enough for you and a friend.

¼ cup dried parsley
2 tablespoons marjoram
1½ tablespoons thyme
1 teaspoon chervil
2 bay leaves
1 tablespoon celery seed

Combine and stir well. Crumble bay leaves for even distribution. Split among 24 4-inch squares of cheesecloth, then tie each firmly with white string. Store until used.

Makes 24.

Handy Hint: Warm milk will make you sleepy. Calcium is a calming mineral. Any high calcium food will relax the counter-of-sheep.

Healing Poultice

A poultice may be cool, warm or hot depending upon the ingredients and the effect sought. The function of the poultice is to apply healing ingredients to the surface of the body to help it. In many cases what is good for the inside of the body will also help in a poultice form. Comfrey is an excellent example, containing healing qualities which work well inside and out at the same time. This poultice is excellent for a wound.

½ cup comfrey leaves (fresh is best), mashed
1 tablespoon wheat germ oil
1 400 I.U. Vitamin E capsule, pierced

Mash the comfrey leaves in a mortar and grind in the oil and vitamin E until all is smooth. Apply directly, or in a cheesecloth to the affected area and leave for several hours. Repeat until the wound is healed.

Note: This combination promotes healing and discourages scarring by causing the edges of the wound to come together. Therefore extra scar tissue, manufactured by the body, is not necessary.

Warm Compress for Aching Joints

¼ cup nutmeg, ground
¼ cup mace, ground
⅔ cup water, or more to cover

Combine the ingredients and simmer up to 15 minutes. Cool slightly, then smear in cheesecloth and apply as a compress to the affected area. Steam to reheat this compress and use a second time.

Massage Oil for Skin and Soul

A good massage depends upon proper friction and improved circulation. Without massage oil, this result is impossible. The secret to massage oil is to use nutritious, non-drying, emollient oils together with an herbal scent which relaxes the massagee. When applying massage oil, always heat the oil slightly in the hands before applying. And to provide continuity and comfort to the massagee, always have at least one hand in contact with the person at all times.

½ cup almond oil
¼ cup avocado oil
2 tablespoons wheat germ oil
¼ cup apricot oil
1 400 I.U. Vitamin E capsule, pierced
1 20,000 I.U. Vitamin A capsule, pierced
¼ ounce oil of lavendar *(Your option here for any oil you choose. Other excellent choices are pennyroyal, carnation, lemon, orange, rose)*

Combine the four oils together and shake well. Squeeze the contents of the two vitamin capsules into the oil mixture, then add the essential oil. Shake well and let stand overnight before using. Shake before using. Makes about 1½ cups. Store in a cool, dark place.

Handy Hint: Hot chocolate in the evening may keep you awake all night with caffeine. Try hot carob drink instead. No caffeine and fewer calories, too.

Herbal Sleeping Pillow

The aromatic effect of some herbs will help one sleep well and deeply. Make a small pillow of herbs and rest your head upon it for a night of sound sleep and a rejuvenation of the spirit for the day to come.

2 ounces rose petals
1 ounce mint
1 ounce rosemary
¼ ounce cloves, crushed

Combine these herbs, crush lightly and fill a cloth bag or pillowcase. Sleep on it. For a more permanent arrangement, custom allows for an embroidered sleeping pillow.

Basic Bath Oil Recipe

For a moisturizing, soothing bath.

½ cup almond oil
½ cup peanut oil
½ cup safflower oil
½ cup wheat germ oil

Combine these oils together in a sealed container and shake well. To it add one of the following combinations:

½ ounce lavendar oil
½ ounce oil of basil
  or
½ ounce oil of bergamot
  or
½ ounce orange oil
½ ounce lemon oil
  or
1 ounce of any oil or essence combination which you want for a desired effect.

Shake well and use 1-2 tablespoons per bath. Store covered. Makes a generous pint of bath oil. (Shaking before each use may be required.)

Lemon-Lavendar Bath Powder

2 ounces unscented talcum or talc
2 ounces lavendar, powdered
½ ounce lemon peel, powdered

Combine these three ingredients and pulverize further. Sift out any larger particles and store in a shaker container. Use after bath and for a cooling, refreshing effect.

Facial Masques for Fast Relief From:

Dry, flaky skin: apply mashed papaya pulp for 15 minutes, then rinse.

Oily skin: make a paste of dry oatmeal and water. Apply 10 minutes and rinse.

Acne skin: honey and wheat germ oil combination rubbed into skin for nutritive healing and cleansing. Leave 15 minutes, then rinse.

Flaky, tired skin: brewer's yeast with water to make a paste. Rub into skin briskly, set 10 minutes, then rinse.

Sunburned skin: apply cucumber slices for 10 minutes. Rinse.

Wrinkled skin: apply cocoa butter or coconut oil at night.

Oily, lifeless skin: almond meal, kelp powder, rye flour and apricot oil scrub. Use daily.

Dry skin: make a thick paste of apricot, avocado or banana, mixed with olive oil to make a spreadable paste. Apply to face for 10 minutes, then rinse and pat dry.

Freckles or blotchy color: apply lemon slice to affected area for 15 minutes. Wash, then moisturize.

Blackheads: tomato slices or mashed tomato applied to face for 15 minutes. Rinse and pat dry.

Herbal Facial Steam

To cleanse the pores, soften, refine and moisturize the skin, an herbal steaming is excellent. Simply pour 1 quart boiling water over about ½ cup herbs (may select from the bath herbs listed or make a combination of your own) in a large glass bowl. Cover with a towel and allow to steep for 10 minutes. Easily lift the towel and lean over the bowl. Make a tent with the towel over your head and steam your face 15 minutes. Take care not to steam your face too heavily if the water is not cooled slightly. Rinse your face with cool water and pat dry gently.

Note: the facial sauna is my favorite time to use up little dabs of herb tea in my cupboard. Also, if I use tea bags in this process, I allow them to cool and use as eye packs after the facial sauna for added effect on the eye area.

Carrot Pack for Mumps

Carrots are full of Vitamin A and the goodness of carrots can be taken into the body through the skin. This pack is good not only for mumps, but for other glandular swellings of the same variety. This is also a fun pack or "poultice" that is easy to do and the fast results will show you the benefits of this method of healing.

3 large carrots, shredded

Shred unpeeled, washed carrots and fold into a cheesecloth that will service the subject's throat size from ear to ear. Leave the pack on the gland area for about 30 minutes, or until the color of the carrot shreddings is substantially faded. Discard. This pack may be repeated several times per day as needed for relief.

Fennel Wrinkle Masque

¼ cup water
2 tablespoons fennel seed
3 tablespoons honey
1 teaspoon fennel herb
½ cup plain yogurt

Combine the water and fennel seed and boil 10 minutes. Strain and combine infusion with honey, fennel herb and yogurt. Mix well, let stand 5 minutes, then apply to the face and neck. Let stay on the face 15 minutes, then remove and wash with tepid water. Gently pat dry.

Herbal Beauty Baths

Adding herbs or decoctions to the bath is a very ancient and effective way to obtain results from healthful herbs. Combine ½ cup herb (from the listing below, singularly or in combination) in a nylon stocking, wash cloth or other fabric container and fasten it under the running faucet of a hot bath. When the tub is full, drop bag into the water for further effect. (For maximum effect, boil herbs in 2 quarts water for 15 minutes prior and add the decoction, plus the herb bag to the bath.) Select the effect you desire and use herbs in your bathwater.

Antiseptic: lavendar, thyme, peppermint, eucalyptus, wintergreen

Astringent: sage, comfrey root, strawberry leaves

Calming: valerian, balm, marjoram, hops, catnip

Healing: peppermint, camomile, elder flowers, rosemary

Moisturizing: orange blossoms, camomile, rose petals, rose hips

Softening: fennel, rose petals, elder flowers

Improved circulation: thyme, lavendar, rosemary

Potpourri

Potpourri is traditionally a mixture of dried flowers, herbs and spices which give a sustained scent to the area around it. A potpourri will keep a room, closet, hallway or kitchen smelling fresh and sweet for years. Traditionally the potpourri begins with a base of dried rose petals, to which other items are added. Experiment for the combination you enjoy most.

Rose-Lavendar Potpourri

10 ounces rose petals
10 ounces lavendar
5 ounces sweet rose buds
2 ounces orris root, ground
¾ ounce crushed cinnamon bark
½ ounce allspice
½ ounce clove
10 tonka beans, ground

Combine and toss lightly. Display in an open dish or crock.

Lovely Mint Potpourri

1 pint peppermint leaves
1 pint thyme
1 pint lavendar
1 tablespoon coriander, crushed
1 tablespoon cloves, crushed
1 tablespoon nutmeg, ground
2 tablespoons caraway, crushed
1 tablespoon gum benzoin, crushed

Combine and toss lightly. Display in an open container or crock.

Handy Hint: Slices of cucumber will relieve severe sunburn. Follow with aloe vera gel.

Rosemary Potpourri

1 dry quart rose petals
1 dry quart lemon verbena, crushed
1 pint rose geranium leaves
1 pint rosemary leaves, lightly crushed
1 tablespoon dried and crushed orange peel
2 tablespoons gum benzoin
2 tablespoons orris root, powdered
½ cup angelica root, cut
½ cup cinnamon, nutmeg and ginger root combination
½ teaspoon mixed rosemary oil and tonka oil

Combine and toss together the first five ingredients. Combine the benzoin and orris root together, then add to tossed ingredients along with remaining items. Toss well and display in an open container or crock.

Legendary Hungary Water Potpourri

4 ounces rosemary leaves
2 ounces orange blossoms
2 ounces mint leaves
2 ounces calamus, crushed
2 ounces vetiver, crushed
3 ounces rose petals
3 ounces dried lemon peel, crushed
2 teaspoons Hungary Water cologne (optional)

Combine and display in an open container.

Sachet

Sachet is made of powdered herbs which are wrapped in small bags of silk and meant to be with clothes for the winter, linens, in closets or other places you wish to keep fresh or free of insects. Silk is used for its tight weave, since the ingredients are reduced to fine powder.

Excellent Winter Sachet:

8 ounces rosemary
8 ounces mint leaves
4 ounces thyme
2 tablespoons cloves, ground

Combine these four ingredients and crush to a coarse powder. Age in a covered container for two weeks, then sew into sachets. Store with winter furs and woolens for a moth-free wardrobe.

Lemon Verbena Sachet

1 pound dried lemon peel, ground fine
2 teaspoons oil of lemon grass
1 tablespoon oil of lemon peel
1 ounce oil of bergamot
1 pound orris root, ground

Combine and grind together until well mixed. Age two weeks in a closed glass container, then sew into silk bags for a very refreshing, clean sachet effect.

Note: This sachet is particularly effective in the spring. During and after spring cleaning, hang a few sachets around the house for that added clean smell which lemon imparts.

Handy Hint: When adding spices that must be removed later, use a tea ball.

U.S. and Metric Measurements

Approximate conversion formulas are given below for commonly used U.S. and metric kitchen measurements.

Teaspoons	x	5	= milliliters
Tablespoons	x	15	= milliliters
Fluid ounces	x	30	= milliliters
Fluid ounces	x	0.03	= liters
Cups	x	240	= milliliters
Cups	x	0.24	= milliliters
Pints	x	0.47	= liters
Dry pints	x	0.55	= liters
Quarts	x	0.95	= liters
Dry quarts	x	1.1	= liters
Gallons	x	3.8	= liters
Ounces	x	28	= grams
Ounces	x	0.028	= kilograms
Pounds	x	454	= grams
Pounds	x	0.45	= kilograms
Milliliters	x	0.2	= teaspoons
Milliliters	x	0.07	= tablespoons
Milliliters	x	0.034	= fluid ounces
Milliliters	x	0.004	= fluid ounces
Liters	x	34	= fluid ounces
Liters	x	4.2	= cups
Liters	x	2.1	= pints
Liters	x	1.82	= dry pints
Liters	x	1.06	= dry quarts
Liters	x	0.91	= dry quarts
Liters	x	0.26	= gallons
Grams	x	0.035	= ounces
Grams	x	0.002	= pounds
Kilograms	x	35	= pounds
Kilograms	x	2.2	= pounds

Temperature Equivalents

Fahrenheit	−32	x5	÷9	= Celsius
Celsius	x9	÷5	+32	= Fahrenheit

U.S. Equivalents

1 teaspoon	= 1/3 tablespoon
1 tablespoon	= 3 teaspoons
2 tablespoons	= 1 fluid ounce
4 tablespoons	= 1/4 cup or 2 ounces
5-1/3 tablespoons	= 1/3 cup or 2-2/3 ounces
8 tablespoons	= 1/2 cup or 4 ounces
16 tablespoons	= 1 cup or 8 ounces
3/8 cup	= 1/4 cup plus 2 tablespoons
5/8 cup	= 1/2 cup plus 2 tablespoons
7/8 cup	= 3/4 cup plus 2 tablespoons
1 cup	= 1/2 pint or 8 fluid ounces
2 cups	= 1 pint or 16 fluid ounces
1 liquid quart	= 2 pints or 4 cups
1 liquid gallon	= 4 quarts

Metric Equivalents

1 milliliter	= 0.001 liter
1 liter	= 1000 milliliters
1 milligram	= 0.001 gram
1 gram	= 1000 milligrams
1 kilogram	= 1000 grams

Notes

Index

Al Dente, 68
Appetizers
   Beer-Batter Onion Rings, 39
   David's Add-a-Dabba Dip, 42
   Don't Change It Dip, 42
   Easy Spring Rolls, 38
   Heavenly Hommus, 41
   Hot, Tropical Cheese Delights, 40
   Jalapeno Bean Dip, 89
   Karly's Guac Sticks, 38
   Oysters Nevalle, 38
   Shrimp Won Ton, 40
   Summer Toothpick Salad, 41
   Taco Pyramid, 39
   Tuxedo Crab Spread, 42
   Vegetable-Shrimp Dip, 42
Avocado, keeping fresh, 19
Baby Foods, making, 19
Baking Powder, making, 23
Bath, Beauty
   Herbal Beauty Baths, 149
Bath Oil
   Basic Bath Oil Recipe, 148
Bath Powder
   Lemon-Lavendar Bath Powder, 148
Beef Jerky, 30
Beverages
   Avocumber Dilly Delight, 44
   Classic Papaya Smoothie, 43
   Hard Cider Cocktail, 44
   Heather's Graduation Punch, 45
   Naughty Nectarine Smoothie, 45
   Sweet Berry Wine Punch, 43
   The Grand O.J., 43
   Vegetarian Frappe, 44
   Watermelon Chablis Spritzer, 44
Blackstrap Molasses, 34
Bouquet Garni, 146
Bran, 33
Breadmaking, 10
Breadmaking Formula, 11
Bread, Quick
   Authentic Boston Brown Bread, 121
   Classic Banana Bread, 127
   Festive Carrot-Zucchini Bread, 122
   Harvest Pumpkin Fruit Bread, 126
   Holiday Date Nut Bread, 127
   Lively Corn Bread, 119
   Mellow Squash Bread, 123
   My Reliable Shortcake, 124
   Quick-Stir Orange Sesame Dinner Loaf, 129
   Tartan Fruit Scones, 126

Bread, Yeast
   Banana Bran Muffins, 121
   Classic Struedel Dough, 121
   Crunchy Seven Grain Bread, 118
   New Old Country Croissants, 125
   Old Country Pumpernickel, 118
   Pikelets (Crumpets), 119
   Scotch Rye Muffins, 119
   Swedish Rye Bread, 122
   Sweet Honey Wheat Berry Bread, 128
   Whole Wheat Brioche, 123
Butter, improved, 22
   Space Butter, 22
Cakes
   Cascade Carrot Cake, 113
   Dutch Poppy Seed Cake, 114
   Fast and Easy Struesel Tea Cake, 114
   Fruit Smoothie Cheesecake, 109
   Natural German Carob Cake, 108
   Raw Apple Cake, 106
   Spicy Applesauce Cupcakes, 120
Candy
   Confetti Popcorn Balls, 132
   Jungle Balls, 132
Candied Fruit, 14
Canning, 13
   Canning, fruits, 12
   Canning, syrups, 12-13
   Canning, vegetables, 14
Carob, 36
   Carob conversion, 36
   Carob syrup, 36
Cereal
   Golden Breakfast Granola, 124
Cheese
   Yogurt Cheese Making, 21
   Cream Cheese Making, 21
Cold-pressed oils, 34
Compress
   Carrot Pack for Mumps, 149
   Healing Poultice, 147
   Warm Compress for Aching Joints, 147
Condiments
   Apricot Vinegar, 45
   Celestial Conserve, 46
   Fresh Cucumber Flourish, 48
   Herb Salt, 47
   Mango Easy Chutney, 49
   Minty Marinated Carrots, 47
   Old Fashioned Brandied Pineapple, 49

   Saucy Nectarine Chutney, 47
   Space Butter, 22
   Watermelon Rind Pickles, 46
   Zucchini Relish, You'll Never Eat Store-Bought Again, 48
Cookies
   Carob Nut Brownies, 106
   Coconut Shortbread, 107
   Easy Does It Spritz, 107
   Grandma's Brown Rim Cookies, 106
   Heavenly Date Squares, 108
   High Energy Hiking Cookies, 116
   Molasses Snaps, 107
   Spicy Applesauce Squares, 109
   Veranda Orange Cookies, 109
Crackers, Croutons, Breadsticks
   Buffet Bread Sticks, 129
   Glorious Graham Crackers, 130
   Golden Breakfast Granola, 124
   Fresh Croutons, 129, 66
   Scotch Oatmeal Crackers, 130
Cream Cheese making, 21
Creme Fraiche making 21
Crepes
   Breakfast Corn Crepes, 128
   Mexican Dinner Crepes, 87
Croutons, 66, 129
Curry Powder, 23
Dairy Products, 34
Dashi, 58
Degrease a Bowl, 57
Dehydrating, 26-30
Dehydration chart, 26-28
Desserts
   Barb's Mountain, 136
   Bourbon Balls, 132
   Cherries Jubilee, 138
   Coeur A La Creme, 136
   Confetti Popcorn Balls, 132
   Dante's Heavenly Bananas, 136
   Indecent-Kebobs, 133
   Jungle Balls, 132
   Luau Sharon's Hot Pineapple Rhumba, 133
   Rhubarb Crisp, 138
   Shimmering Jewels, 138
   Strawberries Sabayon Monique, 134
Dressings
   Classic Vinaigrette, 74
   Creamy Russian Dressing, 75
   Dill-Yogurt Dressing, 74
   Dressing That's A Meal, 74
   Easy Bleu Cheese Dressing, 73
   Easy Dressing For Fruit Salad, 73
   Easy, No-Cook Hollandaise, 73
   Feta-Herb Dressing, 73
   Fresh Spinach Dressing, 75
   Garden-Lush Cucumber Dressing, 75
   Lime-Curry Dressing, 73
   Zesty Tahini Dressing, 75

Donuts
    Applesauce Health Donuts, 115
    Old Fashioned Farmhouse Donuts, 115
Do-pep, 33
Drying, fruit and vegetables, 26
Eggs, 35
Energy conservation in cooking, 25
Facial Masques, 148-149
    Fast Relief From:, 148
    Fennel Wrinkle Masque, 149
Facial Steam, 149
    Herbal Facial Steam, 149
Fillings (see frosting)
Fines Herbes, 146
Fish Drying, 30
    Gourmet Dry Cure, 30
Flours
    Whole wheat flour, 32
    Whole wheat pastry flour, 32
    Unbleached flour, 32
Flour conversion, 32
Food drying, 25-30
Food processor, tips, 31
Freezing fruits, 13
Frosting, Filling, Topping
    Banana Bread Frosting, 127
    Best Cream Cheese Frosting, 112
    Chocolate Whipped Cream Frosting, 106
    Creamy Carob Frosting, 113
    Creme Patissiere (Cream Filling), 104
    German Cake Frosting, 108
    Old Fashioned Strawberry Honey Sauce, 116
Ginger, in yeast, 10
Gluten addition, 33
Gluten flour, 80%, 33
Grain, steamed, 33
Granola
    Golden Breakfast Granola, 124
Guacamole, 71

Herbs
Alfalfa, 142
Aloe, 142
Basil, 142
Benzoin Gum, 142
Camomile, 142
Cayenne, 142
Chive, 142
Comfrey, 142
Coriander, 142
Dandelion, 142
Dill, 143
Fennel, 143
Garlic, 143
Ginseng, 143
Golden Seal, 143
Henna, 143
Jojoba, 143
Kelp, 144
Lavendar, 144
Licorice Root, 144
Marjoram, 144
Oregano, 144
Papaya, 144
Parsley, 144
Peppermint, 145
Raspberry Leaf, 145
Rosehip, 145
Rosemary, 145
Saffron, 145
Sage, 145
Tarragon, 145
Thyme, 145
Vanilla, 145
Herb terminology, 141
Herb tea, 36
Herb tea, brewing, 36
Honey conversion 35
Honey, raw, 35
Ice cream (see Sherbet)
Ingredients 32-36
Jam and Preserves, 13
    Celestial conserve, 46
    Old Fashioned Brandied Pineapple, 49
Juice, 13
Kelp power, 34
Kimchi making, 24

Lemon-Lavendar Bath Powder, 148
Main Dishes
Apple Millet Bake, 86
    Baked Tofu, 86
    Chicken Donburi, 84
    Greek Tofu Pie, 87
    Grilled Snapper with Curried Yogurt Sauce, 80
    Jalapeno Hom Bow, 89
    Kraut Tofu Pie, 83
    Lamb and Vegetable Kebob Dinner, 81
    Mexican Dinner Crepes, 87
    Oniony Omelet, 83
    Oysters Rockefeller Divine, 78
    Party Pesto, 83
    Perfect Fondue, 86
    Pilgrim Souffle, 80
    Salmon Brunch Puffs, 79
    Savory Porcupines, 84
    Savory Stuffed Peppers, 89
    Shrimp Brazil, 81
    Shrimp Jambalaya, 78
    Simplicity Souffle, 88
    Snappy Tomato Casserole, 88
    Sole in Mushroom Sauce, 79
    Sour Cream Chicken Enchiladas, 85
    Sukiyaki, 85
    Tasty, Low-Calorie Quiche, 87
    Vegetable Curry Pie with Pastry, 82
    Zucchini Pesto Trieste, 88
Marinades
    Classic Teriyaki Marinade, 62
    Mainland Luau Marinade, 63
    Minty Marinated Carrots, 47
    Sublime Marinade, 63
    Walnut Marinade, 62
Massage oil, 147
Mayonnaise, making 18
Measurements, metric conversion 152
Meat drying, 29-30
Milk, raw and non-instant 34
Milk powder, 34
Miso, 58
Molasses, blackstrap, 35
Muffins
    Banana Bran Muffins, 121
    One A Day Bran Muffins, 124
    Spicy Pear Muffins, 120
Oils, 34
Omelets
    Oniony Omelet, 83
    Sunday Morning Omelet, 96

Pancakes, Waffles, Crepes
  Breakfast Corn Crepes, 128
  Buckwheat Maple Pancakes, 125
  One A Day Bran Muffins, 124
  Orange Sesame Waffles, 127
  Spicy Applesauce Cupcakes, 120
  Spicy Pear Muffins, 120
  Sumptuous Breakfast Popovers, 124
  Sunrise Pineapple Pancakes, 120
Pasta making, 11-12
Pasta, recipe conversion, 11-12
Pastry
  Classic Struedel Dough, 121
  Fast One-Crust Pastry, 112
  Pastry For Vegetable Curry Pie, 82
Pickles
  Fresh Cucumber Flourish, 48
  Watermelon Rind Pickles 46
  Zucchini Relish, 48
Pies
  Baked Coconut Ceam Pie, 111
  Banquet Kiwi Tart, 110
  Creme Patissiere (cream filling), 104
  Crown of Glory Custard Pie, 110
  Grandmother's Pumpkin Pie (farm style), 104
  Greek Torte, 112
  Mile High Strawberry Pie, 113
  Queen of Hearts Cherry Tarts, 105
  Savannah Pecan Pie, 104
Pie crusts
  Fast One-Crust Pastry, 112
  Pastry for Vegetable Curry Pie, 82
  Standard Graham Cracker Crust, 111
  Standard Pie Pastry Crust, 111
Popovers
  Sumptuous Breakfast Popover, 124
Potpourri, 150
  Legendary Hungary Water Potpourri, 150
  Lovely Mint Potpourri, 150
  Rose-Lavendar Potpourri, 150
  Rosemary Potpourri, 150
Poultice, Packs
  Aloe Sunburn Poultice, 146
  Carrot Pack for Mumps, 149
  Healing Poultice, 147
  Warm Compress for Aching Joints, 147
Pudding, Mousse
  Charlotte's Carob Pudding, 135
  Chocolate Rum Sauce, 135
  Creamy Buttermilk Mousse, 137
  Fast Mango Flip, 134
  Grandma's Brown Rice Pudding, 137
  Honey Mousse, 137
  Pineapple-Coconut Pudding, 136
Puff pastry, 79
Quiche
  Tasty Low Calorie Quiche, 87
  Trusty Timbale, 97
  Working Gourmet Quiche, 94
Rhubarb sauce, 138
Red meat jerky
  Beef Jerky Marinade, 30
Rolls
  Croissants, 125
  Tartan Fruit Scones, 126
  Whole Wheat Brioche, 123
Sachets, 151
  Excellent Winter Sachet, 151
  Lemon Verbena Sachet, 151
Salads
  Antipasto Vege, 71
  Beijing Chicken Salad, 70
  Brown Rice Tabouli, 72
  Fourth of July Marinated Salad, 68
  Fresh Spring Pea Mousse, 69
  Hot Taco Salad Acapulco, 71
  Italian Seafood Salad, 68
  Molded Gazpacho, 67
  Nutty Tropical Fruit Salad, 72
  Osaka Salad, 70
  Perfect Caesar Salad, 66
  Seviche Mazatlan, 69
  Spinach-Nasturtium Salad, 69
  Spinach Sauerkraut Salad, 71
  Sprouted Apples and Oranges Salad, 72
  Tangy Tomato Aspic, 66
  Velvety Avocado Mousse, 67
Salad Dressing (see dressing)
Salsa, 87
Salt, Sea, 33
Salt, Vegetable
  Herb Salt, 47
Sauces
  Chinese Oyster Sauce, 59
  Chocolate Rum Sauce, 135
  Classic Caper Sauce, 61
  Classic Teriyaki Marinade, 62
  Creamy Horseradish Sauce, 62
  Dipping Sauce for Sashimi, 59
  Hot Pepper Oil, 60
  Mainland Luau Marinade, 63
  Old Fashioned Strawberry Honey Sauce, 116
  Pesto, 62
  Red Soy Sauce, 61
  Refreshing Tomato Sauce, 61
  Rhubarb Sauce, 138
  Sabayon Sauce, 134
  Secret Black Bean Sauce, 60
  Sublime Marinade, 63
  Sweet and Sour Won Ton Dipping Sauce, 60
  Tempura Dipping Sauce, 59
  Walnut Marinade, 62
Sauerkraut making, 24
Saute technique, 34
Sherbet, Frozen Desserts
  Fresh Pear Sherbet, 132
  Rainbow Frozen Yogurt, 134
  Raspberry-Currant Ice, 133
  Sweet Plum Sorbet, 135
Side Dishes
  Apple-Carrot Fritters, 94
  Beet-Kraut Side Dish, 98
  Brooklyn Potato Pancakes, 93
  Carrots in Cider, 95
  Dilly Green Beans, 98
  Easy Egg Rolls, 98
  Excellent Egg Foo Yong, 97
  Fried Rice, 95
  Garden Gourmet Burrito, 102
  Greek Cheese Pie, 101
  Healthy Barbara's Green Potatoes, 100
  Indian Dinner Pudding, 97
  Italian Polenta, 93
  Luscious Stuffed Tomatoes, 99
  New Boston Stuffed Cabbage Leaves, 102
  Plain Old Baked Beans, 92
  Polish Potato Pancakes, 99
  Potatoes Anna, 100
  Salmon Croquettes Janna, 93
  Salsa Casserole, 95
  Saucy Stir-Fry Cucumbers, 99
  Spinach Au Gratin, 92
  Sunday Morning Omelet, 96
  Sweet Potato-Apricot Bake, 100
  Swiss Potato Bake, 94
  Trusty Timbale, 97
  Turkey Pastrami Burrito, 101
  Vegetable Tempura, 96
  Working Gourmet Quiche, 94
  Zucchini Confetti, 101

Sleeping Pillow, 148
Souffle
  Pilgrim Souffle, 80
  Simplicity Souffle, 88
Soups
  Continental Shelf Bisque, 55
  Cream of Cauliflower Soup, 53
  Cream of Leek Soup, 52
  Egg Flower Soup, 54
  Fast Manhattan Chowder, 57
  Fresh Pumpkin Soup, 56
  Fumet (Classic Fish or Game Broth), 55
  Green Goddess Soup, 54
  Old Fashioned Tomato-Rice Soup, 53
  Parisienne Onion Soup, 58
  Russian Sauerkraut Soup, 55
  Springtime Radish Soup, 57
  Standard Quick Stock, 58
  Succotash Corn Chowder, 52
  Terry's Oyster Stew, 56
  Vegetable Stock, 58
  Viennese Barley Soup, 54
  Whole Protein Yellow Split Pea Soup, 52
Sour cream making, 21-22
Spirulina
  Healthy Barbara's Green Potatoes, 100
Spring tonic (see Blackstrap Molasses), 35
Sprout chart, 16-17
Sprouts, 15
Sprouting, 15

Tofu
  Baked Tofu, 86
  Charlotte's Carob Pudding, 135
  Greek Tofu Pie, 87
  Kraut Tofu Pie, 88
Tofu, making 22-23
Toppings (see frosting)
Waffles
  Orange Sesame Waffles, 127
Wheat germ, 33
Whey, 21
White flour enrichment, 32
Whole grains, 33
Whole grain flours, 32
Yeast, 10
Yogurt, 20
Yogurt, making 20
Yogurt cheese making 21

Notes

Notes

Notes

Notes

Notes

Notes

Notes

Notes

Notes

Notes

Notes